# Shaping the Future
of Mental Health Care

# Shaping the Future
## of
# Mental Health Care

*edited by:*
Robert J. Westlake

Ballinger Publishing Company ● Cambridge, Mass.
*A Subsidiary of J.B. Lippincott Company*

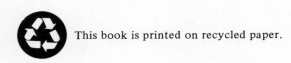 This book is printed on recycled paper.

International Standard Book Number: 0-88410-133-9

Library of Congress Catalog Card Number: 76-3437

Printed in the United States of America

**Library of Congress Cataloging in Publication Data**

Main entry under title:

Shaping the future of mental health care.

Papers presented at a symposium held at Butler Hospital, Providence, R.I., Spring 1975.
Bibliography: p.
1. Mental health planning—Congresses. 2. Mental health services—Finance—Congresses. 3. Mental health services—United States—Congresses.
I. Westlake, Robert J. [DNLM: 1. Community mental health services—United States—Congresses.
2. Insurance, Psychiatric—United States—Congresses.
3. Health and Welfare planning—United States—Congresses. WM30 S529 1975]
RA790.A1S52 362.2'0973 76-3437
ISBN 0-88410-133-9

# Contents

# Preface

In the fall of 1974, a group in the Section of Psychiatry and Human Behavior at Brown University and Butler Hospital met to begin planning a symposium on a topic of national interest in the field of psychiatry. It was the unanimous opinion of the committee that there was no more important and pressing issue facing the field than that of evolving public policy and financing mechanisms for the distribution of mental health services.

This volume presents the formal papers delivered at the resulting symposium, which was titled "Shaping the Future: Funding and Planning for Mental Health Care" and held in the Spring of 1975. The two-day symposium was designed to involve speakers—including health care providers, consumers, third-party payers, representatives of professional groups, and federal health care legislators—representing all of the major areas in mental health funding and policy making. In addition, one speaker was included to compare the provision of mental health services in a socialized country with that in our current system. The program was moderated by the President of the American Psychiatric Association, Dr. Judd Marmor, whose broad grasp of the issues and excellent leadership contributed greatly to making the symposium an exciting and well focused interdisciplinary exchange.

The edited papers are presented here along with an introductory chapter in which I have tried to give an overview of the problem. Space did not permit the inclusion of the discussion periods and the provocative questions posed by the symposium's several hundred participants who attended from twenty states and Canada.

As the discussants' comments have not been published, I would like to acknowledge their important contribution to the symposium. Dr. Joseph J. Bevilacqua, Director of the Department of Mental

Health, Retardation, & Hospitals of the State of Rhode Island joined the panel at the end of the first day and contributed many interesting comments from the point of view of a state mental health executive. Dr. Frank Sullivan, a Rhode Island psychiatrist and Chairman of the APA's Committee on Peer Review, gave many helpful suggestions during the symposium's planning period and joined the panel at the end of the first day to answer questions and comment upon the evolving role of utilization review mechanisms. Mr. Caesar A. Giolito, Director of Government Relations for the American Psychiatric Association, joined the panel for the summation and final discussion period. Mr. Giolito gave much valuable assistance throughout the planning of the symposium and contributed a great deal to the discussion period through his extensive knowledge of trends in health care legislation.

I would also like to acknowledge the generous assistance of the Butler Hospital Grand Rounds Committee, including Mrs. Mulzer, Miss Walker, Mrs. Moore, Dr. Braden, Dr. Rosen, Dr. Fink, Mr. Babbitt and Miss Hostetler whose efforts contributed greatly to the success of this symposium and the Butler Hospital Administration which provided the facilities and support necessary for this undertaking. I would also like to thank Ben W. Feather, M.D., Executive Director of Butler Hospital, for his personal advice and support in the preparation of this program.

I am also greatly indebted to Dr. D. Robert Fowler, Dr. Frank Sullivan, and Mr. Caesar Giolito for their thoughtful review of my introductory chapter and to Mrs. Carolyn Barlow for her tireless efforts in arranging the symposium and in the preparation of the manuscript.

It is my hope that the symposium and its distribution via this volume to a wider audience will in some way contribute to a rational solution of the serious health care delivery problem with which our nation is currently struggling.

Robert J. Westlake, M.D.

# Foreword

*Judd Marmor* *

It is particularly fitting that Butler Hospital, so rich in psychiatric tradition, founded in the same year as the American Psychiatric Association, and whose first superintendent was Isaac Ray, one of the founding fathers of that Association, should be the setting for the symposium on Planning and Funding for Mental Health Care. The American Psychiatric Association, from its inception, has considered its primary purpose to be that of advocate for better mental health care for all Americans. In recent years, under the "right-to-treatment" doctrine, adequate care has come to be recognized not as a privilege of wealth, but as an obligation of an enlightened society to all its members. Nevertheless, psychiatric treatment continues to be unaccessible to substantial numbers of our fellow citizens because they are unable to afford the cost of such care.

How can a society such as ours more adequately plan and fund mental health services for all? It looks very much as though within the next couple of years some form of national health insurance will be legislated by Congress in an effort to deal with this problem. Should such a program be totally federally funded? Should it be on the basis of shared contributions by employees and employers?

*Judd Marmor, M.D., is Franz Alexander Professor of Psychiatry, University of Southern California, Los Angeles, and President of the American Psychiatric Association.

He received his medical degree at Columbia University and pursued his neurologic and psychiatric training in New York City. He is a graduate of the New York Psychoanalytic Institute, is on the editorial boards of many journals and the author of numerous publications, including his most recent book, *Psychiatry in Transition*. (New York: Brunner/Mazel, Inc., 1974.)

Dr. Marmor was moderator of the Butler Hospital Symposium, "Shaping the Future: Planning and Funding for Mental Health Care" and leader of the discussion periods. His opening remarks are presented here.

Should it seek to build a pluralistic program around existing private medical insurance programs, or seek to replace them under a single unified plan? Above all, as psychiatrists we are particularly concerned that any such plan or plans should incorporate adequate mental health care as well as other medical services. A few years ago, many of the plans before Congress totally excluded psychiatric coverage. Now, however, due to the effective educational efforts of the American Psychiatric Association and other organizations in the mental health field, all of the pending proposals before Congress, to the best of my knowledge, incorporate some provisions for psychiatric treatment.

But how much and of what kind? It is our conviction that in most of the suggested programs, the mental health care provisions are still far from adequate. We are by no means unaware of the fiscal realities that tend to dictate such limitations. But we believe strongly that in an enlightened society such as our own, there should be no priorities that take precedence over the basic human needs of its members. Adequate medical treatment of the sick and disabled, is one of those needs. To fail to provide for such care for fiscal reasons ultimately exacts a much higher price from society in the indirect and hidden costs of such neglect.

It is the hope of the American Psychiatric Association that when some form of national health insurance is finally evolved its provisions for mental health care will meet five basic criteria:

1. A delivery system that is pluralistic and does not rigidly mandate or favor one form of mental health delivery over another. It is particularly important that patients have access to early and adequate outpatient care to prevent ultimate more costly inpatient treatment and this care should be equally available from all qualified providers. There is much to be said in favor of organized settings such as community mental health centers, but there is no sound reason to deny the psychiatric patient the same freedom of choice of treatment setting that is accorded to those suffering from physical illnesses. I am aware of no evidence that community mental health centers offer either less expensive (on a unit-cost basis) or higher quality mental health treatment than practitioners in private office practice. Moreover, it must also be recognized that the availability of psychiatric treatment facilities is quite variable in different areas of our nation.
2. Freedom of choice for the psychiatric consumer. This is inherent in the foregoing comments.

3. No discrimination between participation by psychiatrists as compared to participation by other medical specialists.
4. Treatment that is appropriate to the patient's illness or state of disability.
5. Adequate standards, with peer review of utilization at appropriate stages of diagnosis and treatment. The emphasis must be on insuring excellence of care to the fullest extent that is humanly possible within our present limitations of knowledge.

Needless to say, all of these issues pose difficult and complex problems. It is our purpose here to shed light on these and so contribute to the on-going dialogue that is so essential if sound solutions are to be found.

# Shaping the Future
of Mental Health Care

# Chapter One

# An Overview

*Robert J. Westlake*

## THE PROBLEM

There is an emerging national consensus that health care in America now faces an important crisis. Our 100 billion dollar "health care industry" demonstrates the peculiar paradox of providing some of the world's most advanced treatments and at the same time an accessibility to health care that is in some instances quite inferior. This situation has evolved in our country as a result of a complex series of historical factors, rapid scientific discoveries, social traditions, and political and economic forces. Many other countries in the Western world have for several generations been attempting to develop solutions to this problem. In our country, however, the wisdom of providers, consumers, and government has been to generally follow a philosophy of nonregulation and noncontrol, in which the supply of medical services is allowed to develop along economic lines as might any other limited commodity for which there is a high demand. The resulting situation is what many persons have called our health care "nonsystem." In the absence of system development, doctors have tended to fill in the gap by shaping the system in the manner that seems most appropriate to them.

For the most part, however, doctors have a lack of knowledge and overview of the totality of health care delivery and have a limited interest in this field. By both inclination and training, they have a primary interest in the treatment of individual patients and in the advancement of medical knowledge. As a result, our health care system has evolved as a complex mixture of heterogeneous parts, a great portion of which is made up of thousands of individual practitioners of various specialties linked only by an informal referral system. This part of our approach to medical care has been likened to "the "cottage industry" system of production that existed throughout Europe during the Industrial Revolution. Although in recent years more integrated approaches such as health maintenance organisations, group practices, and community mental health clinics have emerged, some with the stimulation of federal and state subsidies, entry points to the health care system are still difficult for many persons to find, and differences in funding of treatment have resulted in a distinctly two-class system of care.

The problem is particularly pronounced in the mental health area where, until recently, good treatment was too costly for most private individuals and unavailable through most insurance plans. To deal with this situation during the last one hundred years, the states have assumed a large responsibility for the care of their citizens who became mentally ill and who could not afford private care. The state hospitals were developed and dedicated to the goal of providing humane treatment in healthful surroundings, but they have now become so overwhelmed that they often fail to be more than "human warehouses" providing custodial care and isolating patients from their social support systems. Many of these institutions are pitifully inadequate to meet the challenge of modern psychiatric treatment and certainly unable to facilitate the shift to ambulatory treatment that is demanded by current standards and treatment modalities. Although the resident population of state mental hospitals has dropped from over 500,000 in 1963 to less than 276,000 [1] at the current time, the development of ambulatory services has not kept pace.

The mental health service dilemma is further complicated by our basic lack of knowledge about psychiatric illness and, in many cases, an absence of demonstrated structural pathology to correlate with diagnostic entities. Diverse treatment approaches abound, and positive treatment outcomes are difficult to demonstrate. In addition, the individual psychiatric practitioner operates in a fashion that is less efficient than his colleagues in general medicine: the number of patients he treats are relatively few, and the kinds of patients he can handle is limited.

The federal government, in cooperation with professional leaders and state and local governments, has attempted to meet the treatment need by creating community mental health centers and it is estimated that 1,500 centers will be needed to encompass the total U.S. population [2]. These centers to date have been a qualified success, yet the federal administration has recently attempted to terminate financial support. For many persons, there remains the lingering feeling that mental health delivery systems cannot be improved independently of the larger health care system and that real progress awaits a thorough overhaul of all aspects of American health care delivery.

In spite of these problems of accessibility, the American system does nevertheless have many strengths. It has enabled us to capture a large number of Nobel prizes in medicine and to provide a segment of the population with high quality health services and personal relationships with their physicians such as is unavailable in most Western countries. Our medical schools have produced some of the world's most highly trained physicians motivated by a dedication to the relief of human suffering and a striving for scientific excellence. The American public has, in many ways, become accustomed to our current system and to its predominant one-to-one doctor-patient relationship. The traditional modalities of health care delivery have been reasonably comfortable to those who influence public decisions, and there has been a strong reticence to disturb our current arrangement for fear of replacing it with a totally unworkable and inferior bureaucracy. However, viewed in the context of social change in the era since World War II, it becomes increasingly evident that the multiple forces playing upon this decision are now about to determine a major change.

The deficiencies of our health care system are now more widely discussed and better understood. The effect of various kinds of discrimination, including that caused by unequal access to health care or access to lower quality care, are more generally and sympathetically acknowledged. New generations of Americans, more acutely aware of the need for social reforms and more comfortable with new approaches to improving social welfare view the problem with attitudes radically different from those held by their parents.

Even within the health and mental health professions, students and recent graduates are far better educated concerning sociologic and economic factors in the provision of services than were their predecessors of a generation ago. While acutely aware of the need for excellence in scientific advancement, they approach medicine with a broader and more sociologically oriented view and perhaps with less of the independent and entrepreneural set that characterized many American physicians of the past. Medical students are more change oriented and are more willing to be critical of themselves and the medical "establishment" and seem to have a greater sensitivity to their "social conscience." This new generation of professional students shares in increasing number the conviction often expressed by public legislators that health care is a right and not a privilege.

Although spokesmen for various parts of our culture, including the once most resistant professional groups, seem to be converging on the notion of a change in the pattern of health care delivery, there is little agreement upon what form it should take. The literature multiplies with contributions that range from political polemics to difficult and obtuse economic treatises. Special interest groups, while developing a gradual consensus for the importance of a significant change have seemed unable to agree upon a viable series of alternatives. In this time of crisis there is potential for tremendous growth, but also for serious error.

It is of the utmost importance, therefore, that persons who will play a role in the making of these decisions in the coming years understand the interplay of forces and their different contributions. The primary forces in this crisis are the federal government, professional groups, the public and the voice of consumerism, the well-developed American private and nonprofit insurance industries, the institutional providers of health care, and the current national economic and political situation. In the remainder of this chapter, these forces will be briefly reviewed as an introduction to the chapters that follow each of which represents the view of one particular force.

## THE ROLE OF GOVERNMENT

Germany, under Bismarck, established health insurance legislation in the late nineteenth century. England established a program of compulsory health insurance in 1911 and began the serious movement of the government into the regulation of health care provision, which led eventually to the establishment of the National Health Service. The governments of other European and Scandinavian countries have, in varying degrees, also become closely involved in the regulation of health care. In contrast, in the United States, government involvement in health care distribution and especially in the distribution of mental health care and has, until recently, been quite limited.

The notion of national health insurance has been repeatedly introduced, but has failed to crystallize. Following the 1911 start in England, the American Association for Labor Legislation won some victories in establishing state supported medical benefits for laborers injured on the job under the provisions of the Workmen's Compensation Act. However, the public interest in health care legislation waned seriously during the relative wealthy period of the 1920s. Notable later efforts to introduce national health legislation were those of President Roosevelt in 1934 and President Truman in 1945. Although such measures were vigorously opposed by many special interest groups, including the American Medical Association, Congress did in 1946 establish the National Institute of Mental Health, which was ultimately to have a profound effect on the development of the field and on governmental participation. The Congress was clear, however, that the NIMH was not to become involved with the traditional delivery patterns of mental health services and that its major mission was to foster basic and applied medical research. The federal government developed only one significant commitment in the direct provision of health services, and this was limited exclusively to the Veterans Administration hospital system with benefits available only to military personnel.

During the next decade, there was little change in the health care picture, but by 1955 considerable public concern developed over the need for a new approach to provision of mental health services, and Congress created the Joint Committee on Mental Illness and Health. This Commission presented its report, "Action for Mental Health," in 1961, and in the early 1960s, under the leadership of John F. Kennedy, the federal government began to move more broadly into the provision of mental health care. In 1963, the Community Mental Health Centers Construction Act was passed, and this was extended and supplemented in 1965, 1967, and 1970.

In a parallel and massive way, the government moved into the provision of other kinds of health care in 1965 under President Lyndon Johnson with the Medicare and Medicaid Programs. The legislative atmosphere that led to these programs was soon tempered by the realization of significant problems in administrating them and by the realization of the tremendous health costs involved in their implementation.

In the 1970s, government has continued to move into the area of health care delivery, but the direction of its movement has been somewhat different—that is, more concerned with controls and cost containment. While utilization review has long been a part of hospital practice, encouraged by insurance companies, hospitals, and accrediting bodies, it became far more important when the Congress, in 1972, amended the Social Securities Act (Public Law 92–603) to require a more rigorous form of review for Medicare and Medicaid benefits. This new utilization mechanism called for the establishment of Professional Standards Review Organization (PSRO) in each of 203 designated geographic areas within the United States. The establishment of these organizations, which is now well under way in many areas, will have considerable impact on the delivery of both general medical and psychiatric services. This review system forces practitioners of psychiatry and other medical fields to attend to essentially "nonmedical" factors in cost control and will inevitably affect the nature of services delivered and may ultimately alter the kinds of treatments that are made available. While many critics say that the PSRO idea is unworkable and that it is on the brink of failure at this time, others point out that a major benefit could be gained by more rigorous application of criteria and standards to the various forms of treatment in psychiatry. Still others point to the need for expanded utilization review procedures to include the growing area of ambulatory care both in an institutional setting and in the offices of private practitioners.

The American Psychiatric Association, while finding some difficulties with the PSRO law, has established a leadership role in attempting to promote its implementation. Other professional groups have been less positive in their reaction to the law. The PSRO movement, however, has found resistance not only from professionals but increasingly from a paucity of federal funding. Real questions have been raised as to whether this legislation, which was of high priority just a few years ago, will ever receive adequate funds for its implementation throughout the nation.

The hesitation in the PSRO movement, the difficulty in carrying forward the schedule of community mental health center establishment, and the problems in shifting the support of these centers to local communities, causes some persons to raise serious doubts about further direct government participation in the delivery and distribution of mental health care. Such critics point out that the important issues of medical and mental health care cannot be subject to the whims of political bodies and to the rapidly changing political and social climates in our nation.

Our legislators have, however, continued to show considerable enthusiasm for health care legislation. Two recent and far-reaching efforts towards greater involvement include the "National Health Planning and Resources Development Act" (PL 93–641, 1974), now passed into law, and the "Health Manpower Act of 1975," which has been passed by the House and is being considered in the Senate. The impact of these two pieces of legislation will be to establish greater control of the development of health planning and policy in all localities and to attempt by governmentally controlled financial incentives to distribute new medical graduates to medically underserved areas. The degree to which these pieces of legislation will be effective has yet to be seen. Nonetheless, they are visualized as two of the principal building blocks for national health insurance.

Until recent years, most health insurance bills produced had inadequate provisions for mental health care. Currently, psychiatric benefits are being added and most bills include inpatient and outpatient services with varying degrees of limitations and exclusions. Many persons take the position that psychiatric care should in no way be differentiated from other medical care, but others point out that this position is unrealistic in view of the much longer lengths of hospital stay for psychiatric patients and the difficulty in controlling appropriate utilization for psychiatric outpatient services. The nature of the governmental decision-making process dictates that ultimately mental health benefits will be weighted against other benefits with regard to cost and political appeal and that a compromise will be reached. A re-examination of mental health benefits in national health insurance will surely take place in future congressional debate. The dimensions and profile in the government's role in medical services will no doubt be developed within the next decade.

## PROFESSIONAL GROUPS

Physicians and other health care professionals have generally been opposed to programs that would involve the government in the direct delivery of care or in the control of the cost of utilization and care. Although there was a great deal of professional opposition to the Medicare-Medicaid legislation, this soon abated as providers found themselves able to charge a "prevailing fee" for services delivered to beneficiaries of this program. More recently, due to new control procedures, Medicaid fees have been set at lower levels than those prevailing in the community, and the program still retains general professional support.

Within psychiatry there are many divergent views on the role of the government in medicine. The American Psychiatric Association has not been antagonistic to the participation of government in the expansion of services in several areas. The National Institute of Mental Health and the community mental health centers legislation have received vigorous professional endorsement. The community mental health centers legislation has led to an entire movement within the field of psychiatry and the development of an active subspecialty with its own body of literature and its own sections within academic departments. These sections have contributed immensely to our understanding of psychiatric services, and the impact of government in this area of mental health delivery is generally considered to have been very positive. Through the network of centers already established, consultation and treatment are being made available to a great number of persons who would otherwise have been completely deprived of care.

Although psychiatrists have been much less positive about the PSRO legislation, which focuses so strongly on rigidly establishing standards and criteria in an effort to legislate accountability, psychiatry has moved perhaps with greater rapidity than other specialties towards the implementation of this legislation. With regard to the next step, National Health Insurance, psychiatrists have generally recognized the need and have become active in helping to formulate a meaningful policy for the inclusion of psychiatric services in such a bill. Under the auspices of the APA and other professional groups, elaborate studies of psychiatric utilization in current health insurance programs have been conducted and their conclusions made known. These studies have shown that insurance for mental illness is financially feasible. How this insurance should be designed is still a subject of considerable debate.

The American Psychiatric Association has taken a strong lead in developing legislation and in proposing expanded mental health benefits in various national health insurance bills. Although originally most of these bills included little or no mental health coverage, during the period in which the APA has been actively working in this area, most bills have come to include some form of psychiatric benefit. As an example of legislation introduced in the 93rd Congress, the Kennedy-Griffiths Bill provided for 45 days of active inpatient treatment, 20 consultations, or unlimited outpatient treatment by a comprehensive center. The Administration Bill provided 30 days of inpatient treatment or 45 days of partial hospital treatment, outpatient benefits that allow treatment in an organized setting with an upper cost limitation, and outpatient treatment by a private physician with about 50 percent as much coverage as for treatment in an organized setting.

In testimony before the House Ways and Means Committee, the APA formally requested the inclusion of benefits for mental illness in any national health insurance program and suggested a pluralistic delivery system with freedom of choice for the consumer [3]. The profession is concerned that funding mechanisms evolved in a political manner will inappropriately determine the nature of treatment and that matters of professional judgment will become secondary. Whatever direction is ultimately taken in developing a mental health care delivery system, it is clear that the American psychiatric establishment will exert an important influence.

## THE ROLE OF THE CONSUMER

Although approximately one in ten persons will be hospitalized for mental illness during their lifetime and a much larger number treated in an ambulatory setting, the voice of "consumer advocate" groups lobbying for mental health programs is relatively weak, though gradually growing in strength. With a few notable exceptions, persons who have received psychiatric treatment are reluctant to identify themselves and to speak out strongly in favor of better mental health care. One large national organization, the National Association for Mental Health, which speaks for the public welfare in these matters, has shown a distinct preference for the community mental health system and has also favored the inclusion of psychiatric benefits in health insurance policies [4]. The National Committee Against Mental Illness represents another type of advocacy organization that proposes a total insurance program with no discrimination against psychiatric illness.

Labor unions have been quite active in calling for National Health Insurance [5] and in negotiating better mental health benefits. The United Auto Workers, under the leadership of Walter Reuther and the U.A.W. Social Security Chief, Melvin Glasser, developed an innovative plan providing excellent psychiatric coverage and achieved its acceptance in 1964 contract negotiations [6]. Among the union membership, however, it is difficult to identify a great deal of support for the mental health cause, and when care is provided, the utilization rates have been surprisingly low.

In part, the lack of strong consumerism in mental health may be due to the fact that lay groups are at times confused by the difficult technical issues involved and the differences within the profession about the most appropriate forms of treatment. Limited citizen enthusiasm may also be due to a general lack of information about modern treatments combined with public retention of popular stereotypes and prejudices developed in a previous era. The lack of strong public support for mental health benefits may also be related to feelings that the provision of such benefits would be too inefficient and expensive or personal tendencies to deny the extent of the need for such services. The Ralph Nader consumer advocate group made one entry into the field and issued a report that was highly critical of the community mental health center movement and outlined its many faults and inefficiencies [7, 8]. This report, however, has been widely criticized by mental health professionals [9].

Public mental health groups and consumer groups have tremendous power to effect change and to shape and design public health programs. It is clear that while legislators may see only self-interest in the efforts of professional groups to broaden psychiatric coverage, the efforts of consumer groups will be viewed with more creditability and will have more political influence. As we move increasingly toward the resolution of the American health care dilemma, it is important that those citizens interested in mental health find an effective public voice.

## THE ROLE OF THE INSURANCE INDUSTRY

In the years since the failure of governmental efforts to establish national health programs in the United States, private and nonprofit insurance companies have grown rapidly. According to Louis Reed and Evelyn Meyers, psychiatric insurance consultants for the American Psychiatric Association, there are about 1,000 insurance companies in the United States offering health insurance coverage [10]. In 1971, about 130 million Americans had some form of group or individual health policy. Blue Cross and Blue Shield have 74 plans throughout the country and have by far the greatest share of the market with enrollment of about 73.5 million persons. Other insurers include private, profit-making corporations, health maintenance organizations, and private practice plans. Some insurance companies also participate in the large federal programs such as Medicare, Medicaid, Federal Employees Health Benefit Program, and Civilian Health and Medical Program of Uniformed Services (CHAMPUS) by acting as the fiscal intermediary.

Insurance companies began the era of expansion into mental health coverage with many severe restrictions and exclusions. In recent years, there has been a tendency to relax some of these exclusions after studies showing that when generous services have been offered their utilization has not been excessive or burdensome. Although psychiatric utilization in many plans, such as the Federal Employees Health Benefit Plan, has increased steadily as the provisions of the plan have become better understood by its participants, there is evidence in a recent study to show that this trend reached a plateau in the year 1973. Also, supporting data from a study of Canada's federal provincial programs, which cover mental conditions on the same basis as other conditions, has shown that these benefits do not consume an excessive portion of the total medical expenditures and do not exceed 5.4 percent of total payments for all medical services.

As insurers have moved to liberalize benefits, the multiplicity of plans and failure of enrollees to understand these plans has been a major problem in health care provision. Complex "fine print" clauses requiring no pre-existing illness, or excluding alcohol or drug-related psychiatric illnesses, or requiring deductibles and co-payments seem beyond the comprehension of the individual subscriber until the time of personal need arises. Insurance companies are fearful that mental health demands will create a large drain on the company's finances. Insurors are further frustrated by the profession's demand for confidentiality, which complicates the issue of claims review.

In recent years, an interesting national drama illustrating the tension on these issues has been enacted. In the summer of 1974, Blue Cross and Blue Shield announced severe restrictions on the previously quite adequate psychiatric benefits in its high option federal employees' plan. A loud and effective outcry from the profession was accompanied by data demonstrating that utilization under this plan was not excessive and had stopped its increasing trend. The mental health profession insisted that the benefits be reinstated. After a considerable period of negotiation with hearings in Congress, the benefits were reinstated and the coverage continued [11, 12]. Shortly after this victory, however, the nation's second largest federal plan intermediary, the Aetna Company, sharply restricted its psychiatric benefits in some plans, and these have not been reinstated. Nevertheless, subscribers to this plan were given the option of transferring to the Blue Cross–Blue Shield plan. There has been some concern that those persons changing plans to maintain their present level of mental health benefit may skew the utilization pattern and costs for the Blue Cross plans.

At the present time, it is unclear how far insurance carriers will support mental health coverage in national mental health insurance. Their gradual expansion of benefits during the last quarter of a century has provided a researchable population that clearly demonstrates it is economically feasible to provide complete coverage for psychiatric illness. These companies, however, are acutely aware of the inflation of medical costs and sensitive to any increases in their total policy cost. While psychiatric benefits may be a relatively small proportion of costs for all conditions, the companies must ultimately rely on marketing influences to determine exclusion or inclusion of such benefits. For these reasons and also because new state laws are requiring all carriers to provide psychiatric benefits, it is likely that the insurance companies will exert a pressure toward the inclusion of psychiatric benefits with day and/or dollar limits, which would provide them with an easy means of cost containment. It is hoped that the continual interplay that exists between insurers, providers, and consumers will result in a gradual and constructive liberalizing of the provisions and the development of a nondiscriminatory policy toward emotional illness.

## THE ROLE OF PSYCHIATRIC INSTITUTIONS

Historically, the responsibility for the treatment of psychiatric illness, much like that for tuberculosis, was seen to fall in the realm of state government. New treatments and changing societal attitudes toward psychiatric illness have now made it possible to provide treatment in more diverse settings—that is, not only in large state hospitals, but also in general hospitals, private psychiatric hospitals, community mental health centers, half-way houses, nursing homes, and a variety of innovative treatment facilities. As the census of most state mental hospitals has been dramatically reduced, the question has been raised throughout the country as to whether these hospitals can be completely closed and all hospitalizations shifted to the private sector, thereby reducing or eliminating the dual standard of psychiatric care.

Many argue that this goal is unrealistic and the state hospitals will have to remain a part of the mental health system to care for the chronically ill who cannot be adequately provided for under the provisions of a national health insurance act. Some reformers have discovered significant resistance to any major change within the state system, and it is often argued that political problems would make it impossible to do away with all of these programs. Some localities that have followed the trend of deinstitutionalization have also encountered difficulties in developing suitable alternative treatment settings and ambulatory treatment programs.

One popular approach seems to be to increase the public role in decision making and to allow public boards to decide which institutions to utilize. Another approach is to incorporate the state hospitals in the development of regional community mental health centers. In this process, inpatient services are better integrated with outpatient and day care services and the population is better served. However, it is difficult to see how the state hospital system would survive if national health insurance allowed patients essentially free choice of treatment facility for acute psychiatric problems, although it is conceivable that these facilities could be partially utilized for patients receiving only custodial care.

There are approximately 175 private psychiatric hospitals in this country; these facilities have a total capacity of about 18,000 beds and are able to provide a high standard of care. Once available primarily to the financially advantaged, this care is increasingly available to low- and middle-income families through third-party payment. Under national health insurance these hospitals will receive an increasing share of the mental health dollar but without rapid expansion they could not accommodate the numbers of persons who might seek their services under a free-choice system. Private hospitals have been greatly involved in the continuing dialogue with third-party payers over issues of benefits provided and insurance coverage. It is in this dialogue that we have seen most clearly the control of therapeutic modalities by the payment mechanism.

As a striking example of this, Blue Cross recently developed an extensive series of "guidelines for interpreting medical information for nervous and mental claims" for use in the federal employees' program (FEP) [13]. In these "guidelines," the authors establish by fiat a single approved form of psychiatry that they term "medical psychiatry" and bar from payment claims involving a wide variety of other treatments that are well accepted within the profession as appropriate and efficacious. Although these "guidelines" have been much criticized, they apparently still represent the nucleus for review of claims by FEP patients treated in private psychiatric hospitals.

In addition to nonprofit private facilities, there are numerous proprietary psychiatric hospitals that offer psychiatric treatment. In recent years, some of these, which have managed to take full advantage of the insurance payment structure, have generated a great deal of criticism. They respond, however, that they are able to offer a high level of psychiatric treatment and that they are consistently selected by consumers who operate in a market in which many choices are available. How these proprietary facilities would fare under a national health insurance program and whether their profits would be in any way controlled is yet unclear.

General medical hospitals, which once almost completely excluded the treatment of psychiatric disorders, are increasingly encouraging the admission of psychiatric patients and developing psychiatric inpatient services. It is quite likely that this form of care will continue to increase with government intervention in health care distribution. The psychiatric care in a general hospital is often more attractive to consumers because it has a lessened stigma and represents a radical departure from the old state hospital image. Psychiatric treatment in general hospitals is attractive to insurors because it has traditionally provided a shorter length of hospital stay and more easy cost containment. The addition of psychiatric units has also been attractive to general hospitals themselves because the high utilization and relatively low operational cost of these units provides relief from the increasing financial pressures imposed by rigorous medical-surgical utilization review procedures. In addition, many persons within the profession feel general hospital psychiatric treatment is preferable because many treatments in psychiatry are now more organically based and psychiatrists work in closer relationship with their medical-surgical colleagues. The comparison of general and specialty hospitals is further complicated by the emerging consensus that they do not treat the same kinds of emotionally ill patients and that the patients treated by psychiatric hospitals are generally more difficult to treat and require more intense intervention over a longer period of time.

The role of general and state hospitals in the provision of ambulatory psychiatric care is quite small. Ambulatory care has heretofore been rendered primarily by private practitioners and community clinics. In several national health insurance bills put before Congress, there has been a systematic bias favoring ambulatory care delivered in an "organized setting." It is possible that this notion will be reflected in national health legislation and that hospitals and institutions may come to play a larger role in the provision of ambulatory care.

Whatever direction is finally assumed in national legislation, it is clear that the existing psychiatric institutions have a large stake and will play a large role. State hospital systems will probably not disappear and it is hoped that their substantial resources and facilities can be constructively harnessed in the provision of upgraded psychiatric services. General hospitals and private psychiatric hospitals will probably expand their services but their relative share of the market has yet to be determined. Legislation could distinctly favor one type of facility over the other through the mechanism of economic incentives. In such control, there is a clear danger, however, that the development of innovative and cost-effective facilities will be inhibited. The institutions themselves will ask for psychiatric coverage of emotional illness on a par with any other medical condition but in fact will probably have to be content with less extensive coverage. In any case, the role of the existing institutions will be important and the final provisions of a national health insurance program may to some degree involve a public and political assessment of the past performance and future potential of these institutions.

## THE ECONOMIC SITUATION

That health care economics exist within a larger socioeconomic field is a potent factor that will affect the ultimate determination of any health legislation. Considerations of national health insurance have arisen historically at times of national financial crisis and have seemed less pressing in times of prosperity. Eras of inflation, economic recession, and high unemployment raise public interest in federal support for health care, but temper enthusiasm for the required massive federal spending.

The rapid growth of medical costs under Medicare and Medicaid and difficulties in controlling these costs in the face of limited supply, expanding demand, and monopolistic market practices raises serious questions about the economic feasibility of a large-scale national health insurance program. These questions have undoubtedly inhibited the introduction of such a program to date and many persons are clearly concerned that a large degree of federal participation in health care would be inefficient, financially deleterious to the country, and raise taxes to a level that would be unacceptable to most citizens. In this vein, a recently retired secretary of HEW has suggested that the further growth of our social welfare programs could undermine the nation's economy and destroy the free enterprise system. The lessons of Medicare and Medicaid have suggested that such programs help to create inflationary pressures by raising the demand for services that are limited. Some observers suggest that this is due to a limited supply of providers while others point to a low efficiency in the output of the provider system because of inefficient organization and overlapping services. It is probable that legislation will attack both the supply and efficiency questions while unquestionably raising the demand for services.

Economic forces will ultimately play an important if not decisive role in the shaping of mental health care services available under national programs. Although the total mental health cost would be a small proportion of costs for all conditions the inclusion of mental health benefits is somewhat more questionable and open to public debate than the inclusion of benefits for medical and surgical illnesses. The political process may conclude that some other form of specialty care is more necessary and appealing to the public and that mental health services must be severely limited so that other more "popular" benefits may be expanded. Also, if our current economic climate does not appreciably improve, the scope of our national health legislation may be significantly narrowed or the total program may be further postponed.

Physician's personal economic systems must also be considered, and health care planners must thoroughly understand our current pluralistic health care system and some of its more subtle operational aspects. If, for example, planners design a system in which all physicians are presumed to operate exclusively at the control of economic incentives, they may be considerably surprised to find that they have omitted some of the major forces motivating the majority of health care providers. Although economic incentives are clearly important, it seems clear that few physicians would place them as primary in motivating their professional efforts. A system that did not somehow allow for the broad range of factors in professional motivation might create a serious loss of professional morale and have a strong negative effect on the quality of medical care.

The institution of proper health reform measures will unquestionably require a great deal of understanding of the dynamics of the health care system and a timely integration in the overall economic picture of the nation. Were it not for our current economic uncertainty, we would probably now have a national health act. This faltering of the economy has given mental health professionals an opportunity to promote the cause of expanded coverage for emotional illness. It remains to be seen what effect the economic picture will have on the final inclusion of such benefits.

## CONCLUSION

This chapter has presented an overview of the major forces in the current national health care debate. These forces include professional groups, consumer advocate groups, the health insurance industry, institutional providers of mental health care, and national economic trends. It is impossible to predict the outcome of the interaction of these heterogeneous influences, but it is certain that our American system will provide a political solution and it is important that we understand the options so that we may contribute constructively to that solution.

## NOTES TO CHAPTER ONE

1. Bachrach, Leona L., *Psychiatric Bed Needs: An Analytical Review National Institute of Mental Health, Mental Health Statistics Series D, No. 2* (Washington, D.C.: U.S. Government Printing Office, 1975) p. 2.

2. American Hospital Association Advisory Panel on Financing Mental Health Care, *Financing Mental Health Care in the United States: A Study and Assessment of Issues and Arrangements* DHEW Publication No. (HMS) 73–9117 (Washington, D.C.: U.S. Government Printing Office, 1973) p. 56.

3. Gibson, R.W., Kolp, W.D., Reibel, J.S., Myers, E.S. *Testimony Submitted on Behalf of the American Psychiatric Association on National Health Insurance* (Before the Ways and Means Committee, U.S. House of Representatives, April 26, 1974).

4. National Association for Mental Health, "Position Statement on Principles for Mental Health Provisions in National Health Insurance, adopted by Board of Directors, June 19, 1971, NAMH Position and Policy Statement Manual, P a–19.

5. Woodcock, Leonard, "National Health Insurance" *The Democratic Review* (February/March, 1975, Vol. 1, Number 2).

6. Blain, Daniel and Glasser, Melvin, "Breakthrough in Non-hospital Psychiatric Insurance." Scientific Proceedings in Summary Form: The 128th Annual Meeting of the American Psychiatric Association, May 5–9, 1975 (Washington, D.C.: Amer. Psych. Assoc. 1975) p. 194.

7. Chu, F., Trotter, S: The Mental Health Complex, Part I: Community Mental Health Centers (Washington, D.C.: Center for Study & Responsive Law 1972).

8. Chu, Franklin D. and Trotter, Sharland. *The Madness Establishment;* (New York: Grossman Publishers, 1974).

9. Farnsworth, D.L., Marjor, J., and Cole, J.O., "Comment" *American Journal of Psychiatry* 131:7. July 1974. pp. 779–782.

10. Reed, L.S., Myers, E.S., Scheidemandel, P.L., *Health Insurance and Psychiatric Care: Utilization and Cost* (Baltimore: Garamond/Pridemark Press, 1972) p. 58.

11. Hite, Charles, Blue Cross Claim Denials Spur Opposition, Probe, *APA Psychiatric News* Vol. IX, No. 8, April 17, 1974, page 1.

12. McDonald, Margaret, "Blues Call Off Proposed Cuts in FEHB Benefits," *APA Psychiatric News* Vol. IX, No. 23, December 4, 1974, page 1.

13. Blue Cross/Blue Shield Federal Employees Program, Claims Administration of Nervous and Mental Benefits (Guidelines for Claim Review).

Chapter Two

# Development of an Integrated Mental Health Delivery System

*William Goldman* *

To this very day, the mental health "nonsystem" in the United States has been marked by the split between newer community mental health programs and more traditional and long-standing institutionally based services. I should like to illustrate one attempt to solve this problem by describing our efforts in Massachusetts from late 1973 through 1974. During this time, the Massachusetts Department of Mental Health began an intensive process to finally break down this double system and reintegrate it into a single, unified, comprehensive, community-based service delivery system. The fact that this objective had been public policy for nine years and that the task was still incomplete is a significant clue, itself, to the difficulties involved.

Not only had the state hospital system and its proponents maintained their hold on the vast majority of mental health funds, but this situation had itself become institutionalized through a budget and personnel system that to all extents and purposes was engraved in marble. The fact that "deinstitutionalization" had been steadily and evenly progressing for almost twenty years in Massachusetts had

*William Goldman, M.D., is a consultant to many organizations in mental health system development.

Dr. Goldman received his medical training at Tufts University and his psychiatric training in Hawaii and San Francisco. He has been Director of the Westside Community Mental Health Center in San Francisco and from 1973–1975 was Commissioner of the Department of Mental Health in the State of Massachusetts. He has been Chairman of the National Council of Community Mental Health Centers and is currently Chairman of the American Psychiatric Association's Committee on Financing of Mental Health Care. Dr. Goldman has held numerous teaching positions, is a reviewer for several scholarly journals, and has authored many papers on the topics of mental health administration and community mental health services.

in no way significantly altered the structure of the mental health system. The fact that most formally hospitalized patients had moved into the community and that significantly fewer acutely disturbed persons had ever reached a state hospital had not brought about a commensurate redistribution of mental health resources on the part of the state.

Along with this deinstitutionalization process, there had been a steady—though unstable and erratic in the past couple of years—growth in community mental health funds from federal sources. These funds, however, were unevenly distributed and not, in any discernible way, developed according to a rational process or related to an explicit plan. Nevertheless, the federal effort was being enhanced by growing involvement of local governments. Counties, towns, and cities were increasingly providing local tax monies at the behest of growing citizen support for community services. The reality, then, was that the state had lagged in adapting to the fact that the need for additional resources was in the community and that services had already been decentralized. The state had not adjusted to a system in a period of evolution that represented far more than just getting patients out of institutions that had ceased to benefit them, if in truth, they ever did.

The task became how to involve all interested, concerned, and relevant parties in a planned and orderly transfer of mental health resources and program authority from the large, archaic, and isolated institutions to the new community programs. The basic vehicle that we chose for the final phase of this process was the preparation of the budget for the 1975–76 fiscal year.

The 1966 Community Mental Health Act in Massachusetts had established a critical and central role for citizen advisory boards in each of its 39 catchment areas. In fact, however, their actual involvement was uneven and peripheral at best. There was little actual departmental support for the development of a true partnership with the citizens. We determined that there was no better way to confirm our commitment to this partnership than to deeply involve citizens in the budget process. We felt it was equally important to keep citizens accurately and immediately informed on the negotiations and transformations the budget might be subject to as it moved through the executive branch and finally emerged in the governor's budget presentation to the legislature. We also attempted to follow it as diligently as possible through the legislative process. We believed that it was crucial to rebuild a citizen alliance and link the department to a public constituency.

In 1974, the area advisory boards, regional councils, and State

Advisory Council did become involved in the budget building process from its inception through its completion, eight months later. The actual preparation of this budget submission entailed major involvement of thousands of citizens across the commonwealth, not only through the official boards and councils, but also through the mental health associations, mental retardation associations, and other special advocacy groups.

In order to emphasize once and for all the importance of decentralizing program authority to the catchment area level, we delegated the authority for the setting of budget priorities for both existing as well as needed new resources to the area advisory boards. This made concrete our commitment to intimate citizen participation in fundamental decision making affecting their life support services. Briefly, the process was as follows:

In December 1973, the department published, in draft form, program budget instructions. This was the first time that any operating agency of Massachusetts government had attempted to develop a program budget. It was also the first time that the citizens had a chance to be involved in the budget process earlier than one or two months before its completion. These draft instructions requested feedback for refinement. The final instructions were issued in February.

Area boards that worked with local programs and mental health professionals in their communities were requested to submit their initial program budgets by the end of April. These budgets contained a summary of all existing programs. This included data on all funding sources and numbers of people served, as well as a detailed plan for the area consisting of demographic profiles, service gaps, recommendations for change and reallocation of existing resources, and requests and justifications for new programs.

All requests were prioritized and rank ordered and had to be signed off by the area board and then submitted to the Regional Advisory Council. The Regional Council was composed solely of representatives from each of the five to seven areas that represented each region. The Regional Council, in turn, prioritized and rank ordered all the requests they received from their entire region and then submitted that budget to the central office by the end of June.

During the month of July, budget hearings took place in each region with the citizens and staff from each area presenting their requests to top central office staff. This was the first time that this kind of participation and transaction had occurred. Many proposals were disallowed either because funding would be available sooner than for the year being requested or because the program request was the legal responsibility of another agency or funding source.

Feedback summarizing the results of that region's budget hearing area by area was then transmitted in memo form to each area's staff and citizen board. In addition, areas were encouraged to appeal any disagreements with the decisions made at the hearing. There were a few. Two such appeals were subsequently modified; three or four others, which were in conflict within a region, were tabled for later negotiation.

The central office process then proceeded. This final phase was to synthesize the seven regional priorities, and the end product of this effort then became the budget request of the Department of Mental Health for fiscal year 1975–76. Thus, the budget request *emanated from the citizens and staff at the area level and was integrated and approved at the regional and central level.* This point cannot be overemphasized.

Another major consequence of the 1975–76 budget preparation was the generating of significant new data. The process produced for the first time a breakdown of the total mental health resources in each area, which when compiled statewide, allowed comparisons between regions and areas in how mental health resources were allocated. This data was broken down on a per capita basis and was expressly made available to the areas so as to facilitate planning for future resource allocation and priority-setting during the process of budget building for the following fiscal year.

In addition, the new information was organized to show how resources were utilized according to general categories, such as adult, children, drug programs, and legal medicine programs. This arrangement verified and helped provide support for priorities appearing in individual area requests for additional resources, particularly in the proposals to fill gaps in services to children. Despite the marked emphasis on the gaps in children's services, it was encouraging to note that although the majority of areas still spent most of their resources on inpatient care, almost a third did not.

In discussing the 1975–76 budget preparation process, I have emphasized the building of the alliance between the Department of Mental Health and the citizens groups. (As Commissioner of this department, I personally met with each of the thirty-nine area boards and seven regional councils in my first year in Massachusetts.) There are, however, a number of additional important alliances that also require particular attention. One is the alliance between the public and the private sectors. Without elaborating on the question of whether a distinction can be made any longer between public and private, it was significant during this same period to recognize the inappropriately heavy dependence on the state's provision of direct mental health care. This pattern had resulted in the more limited and retarded development of mental health services and underutilization of the private sector. In Massachusetts, contracts for services, which had been recently developed in the early 1970s, were being used primarily for drug abuse programs and community residences for the retarded. Many components of government were suspicious of the increasing trend away from the direct provision of services by the state. This was true for the whole spectrum of human services and not simply confined to mental health.

Very few community general hospitals had developed psychiatric inpatient units, much less a range of ambulatory services that were hospital based. A liaison was established with the Massachusetts Hospital Association. Meetings were held with their newly formed Mental Health Committee and a good deal of effort and encouragement was expended successfully. This resulted in a rapid increase in the development of new general hospital psychiatry units. The rapidly declining utilization rates in obstetric and pediatric units increased the motivation of the hospitals to make use of that space. Consultation was solicited from those hospitals that had developed successful psychiatry programs. Comprehensive Health Planning agencies provided positive pressure to include psychiatric services on hospitals that proposed expansion programs. These programs were rapidly and fully utilized, and the Department of Mental Health developed either contracts or assigned staff to a number of them. We had clearly committed ourselves publicly to a pluralistic delivery system with public underwriting, which accelerated this movement.

Another alliance of note was that needed between the urban and rural constituencies. The mental health care system in Massachusetts had long been bitterly divided over the fact that the greater Boston area monopolized the vast majority of mental health resources and state support. This fact was dramatically reaffirmed with the new data produced by the program budget process. The western part of the state had long complained of being the stepchild of the Department of Mental Health. This was equally so for the northeast and the southeast regions, which also were the more rural portions of the state. With our clear commitment for a more equitable distribution of new resources, a new and more comfortable common ground was built between constituencies.

Significantly absent in the work of the Department of Mental Health were meaningful working alliances with other agencies of government, both within the Secretariat of Human Services as well as other important agencies such as Administration and Finance. Major efforts were expended to develop more collaborative programs with sister agencies such as the Departments of Youth Services, Public Health, Public Welfare, the Office for Children, and Vocational Rehabilitation. Negotiations were also initiated with top finance officials to facilitate collaboration in budget matters and to pave the way for the introduction and development of the program budget. To this end, I personally participated in weekly meetings not only with top Department of Mental Health fiscal administrators and representatives from Administration and Finance, but also with staff from Human Services and later from the Ways and Means Committee of the state senate. This action resulted in an unprecedented working alliance between these agencies in government. This effort was preceded by developing a budget planning steering committee within the Department of Mental Health composed of both clinical and management leadership. These two groups had operated in parallel fashion rather than as an integrated team previously.

The more the above process progressed and the more we witnessed true citizen involvement in the decision making and governance of the mental health system, we invariably moved from a more parochial and narrow view of mental health care delivery toward a broader human services perspective.

In 1973, an attempt was made to reorganize the categorical departments under Human Services into a more functional structure. Though the various departments, with their vested interests, as well as the legislature resisted the reorganization, it seemed apparent that the trend in this direction was both logical and inevitable. Although similar reorganization has occurred in a number of states with varied results, there seems considerable evidence that these systems can and will be debugged. It is interesting to note that a number of states have chosen psychiatrists or other experienced mental health professional administrators to play prominent roles in the leadership of these new departments.

Fundamental to our system-building process in Massachusetts was the identification of the major executive functions that were crucial to the development, support, and maintenance of a modern community mental health system that were either absent or functioning inadequately. In no way was the "Massachusetts paradox" more striking than in this area of administrative endeavor. (When I mention the "Massachusetts paradox" I am referring to the dramatic richness of resources in our field, in general health, in higher education, and in organization and business technology, contrasted with the minimum or inappropriate application of these resources to the public need and the glaring inadequacies of the public service programs.) Among the executive functions most desperately needed were those of planning, monitoring, evaluation, standard setting, and manpower development. I shall elaborate on these and their interplay in mental health system development.

In the fall of 1973, the Massachusetts Department of Mental Health had neither a full-time planner, a planning process, nor a plan. What it did have began in 1972 via a contract and the assignment of some part-time staff in an eighteen-month effort that involved hundreds of persons in a first-stage planning process on the "Mental Hospital and Community Mental Health." This excellent effort under the leadership of the United Community Planning Corporation resulted in a document accepted by the Department of Mental Health, the Secretary of Human Services, and the governor by the end of 1974. This document elucidated the need for and recommended the policies that were necessary to shift from an institution-based to a community-based care system. We then charged this same planning group with instructions to embark on the second stage of the process. They were asked to develop a manual with instructions for implementing the recommendations as well as creating specific guidelines on how to develop comprehensive community-based services. We were able to add new staff as full-time planners to this process while still relying on a contract with the outside consultants as well as the collaboration of many of our key staff. In my letter of acceptance, introducing the manual, is the charge that the planning process continue until the completion of the third stage. The end product would be a five-year plan for the Commonwealth to implement community mental health services for each of the thirty-nine catchment areas. The basic material for this plan consisted of the thirty-nine area plans submitted as part of the fiscal year 1975–76 program budget.

Germaine to all health system planning and central to the dilemma faced specifically by the Commonwealth in its advancement of human services programs is the absence of any governmental mechanisms to deal with obsolescence. This is dramatic when applied not only to land but also to facilities and, perhaps most importantly, to people. As we transform our human services systems from institution-based to community-based programs, the lack of any capacity to translate antiquated resources into modern relevant resources becomes increasingly apparent.

The federal government provides us with a good example for the establishment of mechanisms to effect this through the General Services Administration. The need is critical for both plans as well as procedures. For example, an agency of state government, such as Administration and Finance, could very well develop the capacity and capability to take over all unneeded resources—for example, persons in jobs declared obsolete, similar facilities, and unused land.

Retraining, provisions for early retirement, portability of benefits, job retraining, special transportation allowances and other such mechanisms could insure job security for affected state employees. These efforts need not be stymied and retarded because of historical personnel irrelevance. Similar solutions to the inefficient and expensive maintenance of unused or no longer useful buildings and land is essential.

Another illustration of an executive function that was underdeveloped in Massachusetts was quality control. In 1973, the total capability of the department to monitor its complex service network consisted of one part-time psychiatrist. In July of 1974, we hired our first Quality Assurance Team. This was a multi-disciplinary team composed of a psychiatrist (a former Kennedy Fellow in Ethics), psychiatric nurse, psychiatric social worker, lawyer (especially interested in patient rights), engineer (specially trained in life safety codes), and another part-time social worker. This latter person was also to work conjointly with a new Department of Public Welfare team on reviewing and accrediting mental health clinics and day treatment programs for Medicaid.

The Quality Assurance Team began in-depth, on-site evaluations of total catchment area programs including the area's unit in the state hospital. This focus on the area concept involved the area citizen board from the inception of the review. Each review took several weeks and was followed by a written feedback report by the team and an oral report given publicly to the citizens and the staff. The emphasis was placed on utilizing this process more as consultation and technical assistance than as a regulatory function.

We volunteered to utilize this new effort in conjunction with the NIMH's development of a new site visit instrument. Our team then participated in field testing this instrument. The impact of the process was enormous. The positive repercussions affecting the development of community-based integrated care unquestionably enhanced each of the areas reviewed so far.

Still another example of a missing executive function within the Massachusetts Department of Mental Health was that of manpower development. The department had supported training of psychiatric residents and nursing personnel with over a million dollars per year of direct training funds. In addition, it had permitted many of the state hospitals to utilize salaries for service personnel to pay psychiatric residents. The majority of the direct training funds went to support the training of psychiatrists. Approximately 90 percent of this went to one training center. Almost all of the nursing support went to train licensed practical nurses for hospital psychiatric care. Minor token amounts were available for social work and psychology training, which were provided through federal funds available to the department. Aside from a group composed of the directors of the psychiatric training programs, which met infrequently, there was no policy or planning effort concerning manpower development.

In brief, Massachusetts lacked any rational approach that linked manpower development to the primary functions of the Department of Mental Health as mandated under public policy. In late 1973, a Manpower Development Advisory Committee was formed, composed of two representatives from each of the major mental health professions—that is, psychiatry, psychology, social work, nursing, and the expressive, creative, and rehabilitation therapies. These representatives, which were selected by delegates from every training program, were asked to meet by discipline for this purpose and then on an ongoing basis. Apparently this kind of interaction within and across disciplines had not occurred before. Additional representatives were added specifically from minority groups and the special areas of legal medicine and retardation. With the help of this committee, a process was set up for open competitive applications for training funds. A neutral review and recommendation procedure to evaluate these training grant proposals on their merits was also created.

An informal impressionistic survey of manpower needs was done as the basis for developing a Request for Proposal (RFP). This RFP stipulated the priorities for training of the department. It included certain principles, such as an emphasis on community mental health training in a multi-disciplinary training experience that would more accurately reflect the realities of actual contemporary service delivery. It also emphasized minority training and work with children and the retarded. Fifty-seven proposals were received. Private funds were solicited to enable us to bring fifteen national experts to Boston from all over the country for a three-day intensive review process. For the first time, full-time staff were hired in the area of manpower development and assisted in this process.

The legislature responded favorably to this new approach and for the first time in several years provided some additional training funds to the Department of Mental Health. Clearly then, policy decisions were made that there would be a redistribution of training funds and a change in the previous inequitable and irrational way in which funds were used. It was envisioned that this transition would occur in a planned fashion over the next three years.

The need for licensed practical nurses had long been filled, and there weren't any available jobs for the recent graduates of these programs in Massachusetts. The decision was made to shift resources within nursing training to the masters level and to the development of nurse practitioner programs. The plan also called for all the LPN training programs to be closed by the end of 1975.

With the new monies available and the placing into the new general training pool of some of the funds previously committed to psychiatric and nursing training, new programs recommended by the review process were inaugurated in the fall of 1974 that emphasized the priorities stipulated in the RFP. This process enabled us to bring together a number of previously unrelated programs (often close geographically to one another) into new training consortia. In particular, a major effort in this direction was inaugurated in the western part of the state where training resources were most scarce and most isolated.

We attempted, therefore, to reverse a situation that was based mainly on historical traditions and special arrangements and to substitute a policy of support of manpower development that was rationally related to the service commitment of the Department of Mental Health.

A somewhat different but similar task confronted the department in regards to policy for the support of research. Here, too, close to one million dollars in salary and support for research was funded by the department without any central policy, plan or organizational approach to its development or utilization. Research resources were scattered depending on historical accidents. The vast majority of research support was for basic biological research. There was not, in fact, any one person or place within the department that knew the full and current extent of the research effort. Here, too, new policies were implemented that stated a clear priority to shift resources, as they became available and without diminishing the total research effort, from basic biological research toward applied clinical research and program evaluation research. The distinction was clearly underscored between the need for on-going commitment from the national government for basic research affecting the total population as contrasted with the obligation of state government to finance relevant program evaluation and applied research pertinent to its own mental health care system.

Another example of system change is in the area of personnel. As the largest employer in Massachusetts, with over 17,000 employees, the Department of Mental Health initiated a major overhaul of its personnel classification system in early 1974. In addition to proposing new approaches to obsolescence, we felt that the existing personnel system was archaic, irrelevant, and a bastardized hangover from the old institutionally oriented staffing pattern. It had not been reanalyzed or reclassified within living memory.

The mandate of the reclassification project originated in an agreement reached between the Department of Mental Health, the Bureau of Personnel and Standardization, and the Division of Civil Service; also Federal Civil Service concurred with the belief that such a project would facilitate implementation of affirmative action and equal employment opportunity. The project was designed to minimize problems that existed in the current system, including deadend jobs, lack of opportunity for worker mobility (upward and lateral), and mismatching of actual work performance and official job duties, with special emphasis on the fact that the system is shifting to a community-based program. The strategy employed in the project takes into consideration the fact that the mental health system is undergoing fundamental change, and in moving toward community alternatives, many job titles and functions are out of date. In summary, the purpose of the project was to account for work currently being performed within the whole department, as well as to account for the functions that the changing delivery system would require. This project involved staff at every level within the department, representatives of the unions, Civil Service, and the Bureau of Personnel. It was also directed by a new specialist employed just for this purpose.

The issue of Affirmative Action presented itself vividly and immediately upon my arrival at the Massachusetts Department of Mental Health. The first meeting of the formal leadership group of the department, which was composed of thirty persons, revealed twenty-nine white males and one white female. At my invitation, the Federal Office of Civil Rights timorously reviewed our department and found that we were barely within the letter of the law. The executive branch of the state government was gearing itself up for a new emphasis on equal employment opportunity, and we volunteered our department to be the demonstration agency of government to unlock leadership positions to minorities and women.

The first five persons hired by me included three minorities and two women. These efforts were illusory, however, since these were provisional employees and would not attain tenure or civil service security for some time to come. Class action suits were discussed. The stranglehold of self-perpetuating institutional racism seemed nigh impossible to break. Small inroads were made.

One minor victory came, however, in the area of manpower development. With the priority for minority training clearly enunciated in the RFP, proposals were received replete with good intentions, but lacking all assurances. We insisted on minority trainees or no funds, but we added a "carrot" to "the stick." We established a policy that for every two minority trainees signed up, an additional stipend would be granted. All programs were able to comply and received the reward.

For the first time, a full-time minority Equal Employment Opportunity Officer was appointed in early 1975 and operated directly out of the Commissioner's office. Top priority was given to a complete review and overhaul of the department's efforts in this area. At the same time, the department's bimonthly newspaper included a section on patients rights in multiple languages.

A major means to follow through on these tasks was to create a new leadership structure and to attract new leadership. Many attempts at significant system renovation, reform, and change have foundered by putting "new wine in old bottles." The entire leadership of the Department of Mental Health was in tenured civil service positions with the exception of the Commissioner, Deputy Commissioner, and Chief Counsel. Thus, we introduced legislation in late 1974 to take the top thirty leadership positions in the department out of civil service and have them serve at the pleasure of the Commissioner, which received widespread citizen support.

In late 1973, we also accepted the unanimous recommendation of the State Advisory Council to request in our budget, with high priority, funds to hire new area directors for all the areas of the Commonwealth. The Community Mental Health Act of 1966 included authorization for these top level professional positions, but they were never pushed for by the department. The area director would be the single person responsible for all mental health and mental retardation services for the total population of the catchment area. For the first time, authority and responsibility would be vested in one position. All elements of the area service system, including the state hospital unit serving that area, would be accountable to this person. The area director could reassign or reallocate resources into or out of the state hospital unit as appropriate, so that the resources could follow the patient. Patients in special regional programs would remain his/her responsibility. The area director would be accountable in turn, to both the citizen area board and to the regional administrators for mental health and mental retardation.

This concept had already been operationalized on a pilot basis in 1974 in four catchment areas served by two state hospitals. This shift had been legitimatized administratively and was working successfully.

In 1974, with broad citizen and staff support the legislature appropriated the necessary new funds to hire the area directors. Massachusetts thus made its final commitment toward realizing a true area-based, community mental health care system.

A six months' national recruitment process was then initiated with responsibility placed on the area boards. A clearing-house process was set up in the department's central office to facilitate this and assist with screening the hundreds of applicants from all the mental health disciplines, including Department of Public Health administrators. The mandate for Affirmative Action was vigorously enforced as this opportunity for integration of new department leadership presented itself.

I haven't written the end of this chapter because the story has been interrupted and the end in doubt. What intervened, to put it most simply, was an election and an economic crisis. The process I have been describing has been suspended. I hope it has not been permanently disrupted or distorted. Loss of momentum in the change process and in system building is of no mean consequences all by itself.

In any case, I remain optimistic for the long run. It is ideas and ideals, not processes and procedures, that prevail and the ideals and goals of the community mental health movement are more sound and more needed today than ever.

## Chapter Three

## Society's Attitude Toward the Mentally Ill: The Crucial Factor

*Mike Gorman* *

In tackling the many issues connected with shaping future programs in the planning and funding of mental health care, it is imperative to examine our past experiences—the failures as well as the successes.

As a newspaper reporter who toured scores of state mental hospitals in the decade from 1945 to 1955, I can state categorically that care of the mentally ill was at a frightfully low ebb. The "philosophy" underlining legislative provisions for the care of the mentally ill was a very simple one. They were a hopeless segment of our society, untreatable and incurable and therefore certainly not a medical problem. They were, accordingly, given minimal custody in massive institutions, some of which reached the outlandish proportions of 10,000 to 15,000 beds in size. Because treatment of the mentally ill was a rarity, it was inevitable that the flood of patients would create an incessant demand for more and more institutions. For example, in the decade from 1945 to 1955 the resident population of these human warehouses was increasing at the rate of 12,000 patients a year.

When some argued that the whole system was bankrupt and in need of drastic overhauling, we were told that since the establishment of the first public mental institution in 1773, this had been the

*Mike Gorman is Executive Director of the National Committee Against Mental Illness.

Mr. Gorman is a graduate of New York University and a journalist who has devoted his professional life to bettering the cause of the mentally ill. He is the author of innumerable news stories and several books on the plight of the mentally ill and has been active as an advocate on the Washington political scene for more than 25 years. He is the recipient of numerous mental health awards and is one of fourteen laymen to have been chosen as an Honorary Fellow of the American Psychiatric Association.

*33*

way things were done. Since society rejected the mentally ill, the best sanctuary for them was a haven in the wilderness.

I cannot emphasize this point too often—every reform we have achieved over the past several decades has depended upon the understanding and activism of society at large. The setbacks we have encountered, by the same token, have been due to our failure to modify almost medieval concepts as to the nature of the mental patient.

I think I can state without fear of contradiction that it was the journalists of this earlier era who brought to public attention for the first time the horrible conditions under which the mentally ill existed. Newspaper series by journalists in a number of states brought into public focus for the first time the undeniable fact that we were treating as castoffs hundreds of thousands of people who could be treated and returned to their communities. In a few states there were impressive reform movements, but for the most part they were crisis-oriented reforms—buckets of water designed to put out sporadic fires of public indignation.

The spotty nature of these reforms led some of us to thinking about a broader mechanism that would go to the heart of the ingrained public apathy toward the problem of mental illness. We began working with the National Governors' Conference, and in both 1949 and 1951 they published well-documented studies of a state mental institution system that had outlived its usefulness. These studies led to a National Governors' Conference on Mental Health in 1954, which called for an alternative to minimal and sometimes disgraceful custody of mental patients in the 300 state institutions then in existence.

In cooperation with the Congress, professional and lay organizations in the mental health field devised a Joint Commission on Mental Illness that would take what amounted to an anthropological look at our handling of the mentally ill and come up with pragmatic alternatives to the state institutional system. The report released by the Commission in 1961 laid the basis for the community mental health center system we are engaged in creating today. Following the issuance of the report, the National Governors' Conference held a special three-day meeting to analyze it. The official statement by the governors characterized the Joint Commission report as "the first survey in our nation's history which relates the problem of mental illness to the various responsibilities of Federal, state and local governments."

The importance of this statement should not be lost upon anyone. In very simple terms, what the governors were saying was that the process by which we had dumped the mentally ill in massive warehouses for two centuries was no longer tolerable. This is the kind of societal change in thinking I am talking about.

It took the governors a long time to come to it, but when they did, the attitudinal change had enormous consequences. To quote just one excerpt from the lengthy report of the governors on this question:

> We recognize no stigma attached to mental illness. The treatment of mental illness should be on the same basis as the treatment of physical illness.

Because our concern is with the financing of mental health care, I quote another excerpt that shows another tremendous attitudinal breakthrough on the part of the governors:

> We shall ask our insurance Commissioners to request companies admitted to do business in our respective states to review their health insurance plans with a view to including coverage of mental illness.

This may not sound like a revolutionary statement today, but it certainly was fifteen years ago.

I presume that all of you here are familiar with the culmination of these various efforts—the passage of the community mental health centers legislation in 1963. In essence, this landmark legislation provided for federal, state, and local contributions toward the establishment of treatment facilities for the mentally ill in the heart of the community. However, the societal attitude was again indicated in the fact that the federal contribution to these centers was inadequate and was designed to phase out over a very short period of years. This is not characteristic of most federal programs—the states have been getting ninety cents on a dollar for their interstate highways since 1957; state vocational rehabilitation gets eighty percent in federal matching money year in and year out, and so on.

What are we trying to achieve in the community mental health center concept? It was expressed quite well a few years back in a publication of the Group for the Achievements of Psychiatry:

> We are no longer content to banish the mentally ill to a world that we shun and deny. Instead, with all the unpleasantness, difficulties and trials that accompany professional role changes, we seek ways to bring the mentally ill into the life of the community.

We are not unaware of the financial problems entailed in starting a mental health center with the knowledge that each year its percentage of federal support would diminish until it was finally on its own.

Therefore, following passage of the Community Mental Health Centers legislation of 1963, President Kennedy instructed the Secretary of Health, Education and Welfare to appoint a Task Force on Insurance to establish guidelines for the coverage of mental illness so that mental health centers could survive economically.

Because of its importance, I list the five major recommendations on insurance coverage of the mentally ill released by the Task Force in 1964:

1. Emphasis should be placed upon early referral and short-term, intensive therapy. This would include outpatient psychiatric care, either in a center or in a psychiatrist's office.

2. In-hospital benefits should be increased, and *partial* hospitalization should be included in these benefits.

3. Increased recognition should be given to all professional skills essential to treatment. This would certainly include insurance coverage for the services of the clinical psychologist, the psychiatric social worker, the psychiatric nurse and other skilled professionals working under the supervision of a physician.

4. Insurance should not favor a particular type of treatment. It should not, for example, rigidly insist upon a 24-hour treatment when partial hospitalization is more effective. It should not insist that it will only pay for a physical treatment such as electroshock, while excluding psychotherapy from coverage.

5. Prescribed drugs should be covered for *ambulatory* as well as for hospitalized patients.

The principles were fine, but the actual implementation was something else again.

This did not come as a surprise to me, because for several decades some of us had been battling for coverage of mental illness in Blue Cross–Blue Shield and commercial insurance plans.

As far back as 1954, I testified in Buffalo before a legislative committee and there raised the question as to why Buffalo Blue Cross–Blue Shield had no coverage of mental illness while Rochester, in the same state, had thirty days. The Blue Cross witness said that his plan had sent out a questionnaire that asked the good citizens of Buffalo if they would pay an extra fifteen cents a month in premium costs for coverage of mental illness. They had received an overwhelmingly negative response. Of course they would—who was going to admit he was a candidate for mental illness in the first place, and in the second place pay the ridiculous sum of fifteen cents to prove that he was a potential schizophrenic?

Five years later I testified in West Virginia, and I again raised some of the same questions:

Four of the six Blue Cross plans in West Virginia refused to give you a single day's coverage for mental illness. In Huntington you are allowed five dollars a day for thirty days with only one limitation—you get this coverage only once in your entire lifetime! Charleston Blue Cross does the only decent coverage of mental illness. It allows sixty days at regular benefit rates.

I could pile documentation upon documentation, but you get the point. You just have to consult the various surveys made by the American Psychiatric Association of Blue Cross coverage of mental illness over the years. At a National Conference on Insurance in 1968, I quoted a 1967 American Psychiatric Association survey that showed, for example, that 74 percent of the people of Rhode Island had some mental illness coverage, while only 2 percent had it in Tennessee, and less than 1 percent in Georgia. Further proof of this point I will leave to all of you who should consult *Social Class in Mental Illness*, a classical study of the economics of mental illness by Doctors Frederick C. Redlich and August B. Hollingshead. The essential thrust of their massive study is the extraordinary degree to which lower- and middle-income families are deprived of private and community psychiatric care because of a lack of insurance coverage. The Yale study pointed out that for most families not in the high income brackets, the public mental hospital is the first, and frequently the only, point of contact.

Although we have seen some distinct improvement in coverage of mental illness over the past few years, it is largely concentrated on the in-hospital patient, because the insurance companies and the hospitals only seem happy when the patient is horizontal and quiet. The many other elements of the community mental health center—day care, emergency psychiatric services, ambulatory care and education and consultation—are rarely covered.

The only answer, then, is national health insurance with adequately specified coverage of mental illness.

This assumes increasing importance when we realize that both the Nixon and Ford Administrations were, and are now, dedicated to opposing any further federal support of community mental health centers. States and localities, under increasing pressures, do not have the resources to support a national network of these centers. Furthermore, the insurance industry covers only about 7 percent of the expenses of patients going to these centers.

The present system is obviously unsatisfactory. Some centers at the present time have been forced to adopt eligibility rules and sliding scales of payment that have no justification in an ordered universe. Many centers in low-income areas, both urban and rural, are in a precarious financial position today. Some of them have had to discharge key professional people to keep within a modest budget.

It is our contention that in any national health insurance plan that is finally adopted, mental and physical illness should be covered on the same basis.

Over the past two decades, I have tried in every way possible to convince the insurance industry, which reflects to a great degree some of the public prejudices against the mentally ill, that universal coverage of mental illness was both morally and economically sound. Certainly the massive studies by the American Psychiatric Association in the past few years have supplied voluminous documentation to prove the latter point.

All consumers must be provided the economic means to purchase the psychiatric care they need—not just those who are in the upper-income brackets, who are members of a progressive labor union, or who are located near a modern medical school, or whatever.

I am happy to note that both the American Psychiatric Association and the National Association for Mental Health have worked diligently over the past few years to develop a minimum set of benefits under a national health insurance program. There are some differences in these and other approaches, but essentially their recommendations have been incorporated in the two major national health insurance bills now before the Congress. For example, the Corman-Kennedy bill provides 45 days of inpatient coverage, 20 outpatient visits per spell of illness to a private practitioner, but no outpatient care limits for visits to community mental health centers or health maintenance organizations; unlimited partial hospitalization care in a community mental health center or similar facility; emergency services as provided by hospitals, other organized systems of care and physicians, and aftercare, which specifically encourages one of the most neglected areas in our coverage of mental illness today.

The benefits are somewhat different in H.R.1, which is the American Hospital Association bill, whose chief sponsor is Congressman Al Ullman, the Chairman of the House Ways and Means Committee. It provides 60 days of inpatient care with a trade-off between inpatient care and outpatient care, which provides that the patient is entitled to three days of daycare in lieu of each day of inpatient care in an episode of illness. There are other excellent features of the Ullman bill.

The remarkable progress this indicates is dramatized by one simple fact: in the 35 years following the introduction of the original national health insurance bill by Senator Wagner in 1938, there was no mention of mental illness coverage until S.3 was introduced by Senator Kennedy in 1973.

These are enormously progressive steps, but we must not be satisfied with them as perfection personified. Our ultimate goal is the elimination of all distinctions regarding the coverage of mental illness under national health insurance, and it is my deep conviction that this will come to pass in the not-too-distant future.

As we develop these various programs, we will meet various community resistances.

The latest outcry is the inadequate care we are giving to the mental patients we are discharging from our various state hospitals and, in some cases, from our community mental health centers. Some of these complaints are legitimate, since many of the centers I have visited do not have the social work staff to follow up patients upon their release. However, a great deal of the resistance again gets back to the community's fear and ignorance of mental illness.

In a recent issue of the *U.S. News and World Report*, an article on the mentally ill reported that homeowners and businessmen and many urban communities complained that the existence of nearby halfway houses for the mentally ill "constituted a threat to their lives and livelihoods."

Reading the article, I was reminded of an observation of Doctor Karl Menninger back in the 1950s when the Menninger Foundation took over the Topeka State Hospital. He tore down the cages and bars and opened many wards. In addition, he instituted a policy of visits to the staid and moral city of Topeka. Within a few months, there were the usual kickbacks and the inevitable front-page story: "Escaped Mental Patient Kills Topeka Resident." Several of these stories appeared, and Doctor Karl decided to fight back. He checked the homicide statistics of the "normal" city of Topeka and discovered that the good Rotarians and Kiwanians of that city had a homicide rate five times that of the patients who went downtown to visit their fair city.

I agree with the observation of Doctor William S. Hall of South Carolina, one of America's most distinguished Mental Health Commissioners, when he says:

> The majority of patients can realize maximum benefits in treatment if this can be accomplished close to home, so that a patient will not have to be taken away from the environment he is used to, from his job and from contact with friends.
>
> I feel that treating the patient in the community, or as close to home as possible, preferably on an outpatient basis, is much better than sending him 75 miles off to a State hospital.

As long as you can keep the individual within the community, as long as he is a breadwinner, he can keep the role of a productive member of the community—a generator of tax funds rather than a recipient.

I am not implying that this is not a serious problem, but it will take both funds and, more important, community understanding before we can provide decent care for released patients.

A good deal of our resistance to mental illness in America is due to the almost psychotic way in which we celebrate success in this country. We are therefore impatient with nonsuccess, which we frequently categorize as eccentricity, aberrant behavior or what-have-you.

If we adopted the tolerant attitude that the English have toward the mentally ill, we would avoid so many problems to which I have alluded. For example, in touring the venerable St. Thomas Medical School Psychiatric Unit a few years back, Doctor William Sargant pointed out to me a police sergeant who was hospitalized in one of the rooms. I was somewhat hesitant to ask Doctor Sargant about talking to a patient, but the good doctor and I just walked matter-of-factly into the room. The sergeant told us that he suffered from periodic depressions but that his colleagues understood this and were very kind to him.

The respect for public psychiatry in England is also very impressive. Where our American psychiatrists tend to look down upon psychiatrists who work in public institutions or centers, the British psychiatrists and the people generally look up to these public servants—and this respect long preceded the advent of national health insurance in Great Britain. A community attitude of this nature pays off dramatically. About fifteen years ago, due mainly to economic difficulties, the Minister of Health ordered the mental hospitals to expand their patient population beyond the 2,000-bed limitation, which the superintendents had themselves imposed. The superintendents refused and threatened a mass resignation. They said that any excess of patients should go to the excellent English cottage and half-way house systems. The public backed the superintendents, the newspapers editorialized in their favor, and the Minister of Health withdrew his order.

The attitude is little different in Russia. As a member of the First Mental Health Delegation to the Soviet Union in 1967, I noted that everywhere I went—in the cities, in the countryside, in the factories and in the schools—there was a pervasive feeling that those who had mental problems needed help in the same manner as anyone who had a physical illness.

All the above is not to say that we are not making significant progress in changing the attitude of society toward the mentally ill. I can only cite a few examples:

1. The tremendous movement toward the rights of a patient to treatment. This has become a focal issue over the past decade and is being litigated in many courts throughout the country.
2. The legal rights of a patient, particularly with regard to the nature of his commitment and the right of a hospital to hold him beyond a specified period. The day of involuntary commitment—the standard procedure only a few years ago—is giving way before state legislation and court actions.
3. Better delivery systems that, for the first time, abandon the state monolithic approach and involve the local community and the citizen in care of the mental patient. California offers the best example of this development; it encourages community-based treatment programs by shifting the control of all state mental health funds to local communities. State hospitals, community mental health centers, and other facilities are now integral parts of one local delivery system.
4. The National Association for Mental Health and individual psychiatrists have conducted a long battle for an end to using patients as slave labor in understaffed state mental hospitals. Those hospitals that refuse to pay patients for their labor will have to treat them, and this opens up a whole new vista for improvement.
5. Confidentiality of psychiatric records. This is a very important matter; the American Psychiatric Association, the American Psychological Association, and others have performed effectively in testifying before Congress in making this a major issue.
6. The increasingly widespread movement toward paying greater attention to the psychiatric problems of the elderly. A Boston psychiatrist, Doctor Martin Berezin, has been so effective in bringing this problem to the fore that Senator Edward Muskie has introduced a bill in the present session of Congress for a Presidential Commission on the Mental Health and Illness of the Elderly.

There are many challenges I could list, all of which involve, in the very deepest sense, fundamental changes in public attitude. Attitudes do change, but not very easily. It takes a tremendous effort on the part of both professional and laymen but if the effort is not made, then the individual problems we are discussing here today will not be solved. Until the community truly accepts the new idea, any reform is likely to be ephemeral.

Yet all of this will not come to pass until we take the first steps now. For in the words of the distinguished American philosopher, William Hocking: "The extraordinary thing is this: that all the important things in life are, before they are done, impossible."

## REFERENCES

Council of State Governments. 1949. *The Mental Health Programs of the 48 States.*

Council of State Governments. 1951. *Mental Health Training and Research Programs of the States.*

Felicetti, Daniel A. 1975. *Mental Health and Retardation Politics: The Mind Lobbies in Congress.* Praeger Publishers.

*Final Report of Joint Commission on Mental Illness and Health.* Basic Books, 1961.

Gorman, Mike. 1948. *Oklahoma Attacks Its Snakepits.* University of Oklahoma Press; Book Condensation, *The Readers Digest*, September, 1948.

_____. 1956. *Every Other Bed.* World Publishing Company.

_____, co-author. 1968. *Special Report: First U.S. Mission on Mental Health to the U.S.S.R.* Washington, D.C.: U.S. Government Printing Office.

_____. Soviet Psychiatry and the Russian Citizen in *International Journal of Psychiatry.* November, 1969.

_____. "Community Mental Health: A Search for Identity" in *Community Mental Health Journal.* October, 1970.

Redman, Eric. 1973. The Dance of Legislation. Simon and Schuster.

Chapter Four

# Influence of Financing on the Private Practice Delivery System

*Robert W. Gibson* *

Psychiatry's leadership is being eroded, and unless we can regain a central role in the decision-making process, the future of mental health services will be determined increasingly by fiscal, political, and pressure group interests. The American Psychiatric Association has vigorously advocated equal coverage for the mentally ill under all health insurance. This is essential, but in this chapter the focus is not on the benefits themselves; rather, it is on the critical importance of participation by psychiatrists in the systems used to monitor, review, and control the delivery of mental health services.

Utilization review procedures such as those mandated by Medicare seemingly have not stemmed rising costs for health care. In 1965, the last year before Medicare and Medicaid, annual expenses for health care in the United States [1] totaled $38.9 billion ($198 per person) and amounted to 5.9 percent of the gross national product; public dollars accounted for 25 percent of the expenditures. By 1974, health expenditures totaled $104.2 billion ($485 per person) and accounted for 7.7 percent of the gross national product; public dollars amounted to 40 percent of the expenditures.

Inflation of health care costs exceeded other segments of the economy by claiming a higher share of the gross national product. Even more significant, the public share escalated to a point that health

*Robert W. Gibson, M.D., is President-Elect of the American Psychiatric Association, Medical Director of the Sheppard-Enoch Pratt Hospital, and Associate Clinical Professor at the University of Maryland Medical School.

Dr. Gibson received his M.D. at the University of Pennsylvania and received his psychiatric training in Philadelphia and his psychoanalytic training at the Washington Psychoanalytic Institute. He is an author of numerous publications, has testified before many legislative committees, and has been a leader in defining the psychiatric profession's opinion in the area financing of mental health care.

care became a political issue—indeed a crisis. Under national health insurance, these trends will be accentuated because current proposals would drive the federal tax dollar percentage up to between 60 and 90 percent and would surely increase expenditures.

Increases in the cost of health services are attributable to several factors: long overdue corrections of inequities in the pay of employees in the health care industry; technological advances and increased standards of acceptable practice; increased volume of services as previously unmet needs have been filled.

Misleading statistics have sometimes equated the increases in health expenditures with the consumer price index while ignoring increases in volume as if inflation alone were the cause. The distinction between volume and unit cost is especially significant in mental health where concerted efforts to increase public awareness have increased the demand. Improved coverage for mental health services by private insurance carriers have led to greater utilization of psychiatric treatment. The inclusion of mental health benefits under Medicare and Medicaid as well as federal support for community mental health centers have increased public expenditures. Disregard of these economic forces has led some to condemn increased payments for mental health care as an abuse.

Expenditures for mental health account for about 14 percent of all health services [2], but it is difficult to know whether these figures represent the actual need. Public tax dollars pay for approximately 70 percent of psychiatric treatment and are often arbitrarily controlled by government appropriations. Many expenditures for mental health services are buried in programs for drug abuse, social services, and welfare.

In the past year, statistics have been made available by the largest private health insurance plan in the world, the Blue Cross–Blue Shield plan for federal employees, which covers nearly 4.5 million persons. The relative costs of mental health services in this private insurance program offering comprehensive benefits may reflect the perceived needs more accurately. Benefits in this plan for nervous and mental conditions were steadily expanded in the early 1960s until under the high option plan [3] they approximated the same coverage as for other illnesses (365 in-hospital days per admission, and under supplemental benefits, 80 percent of physicians' charges for out-of-hospital care, subject to a $100 per person deductible).

Quite predictably an upward trend in utilization of mental health services occurred as benefits were expanded. This seems to have ended; in 1964, benefits for mental disorders under the high option [4] constituted 7.2 percent of benefits for all conditions, compared with 7.3 percent in 1973; and supplemental benefits for mental disorders held steady at 38.4 percent in 1973, compared with 38.7 percent in 1972. Inpatient utilization was not excessive; 80 percent of the persons who received inpatient care for mental illness were released within thirty days and only 3 percent were hospitalized for more than ninety days.

Despite reasonable explanations for increases in the costs of health care, serious criticisms have been directed at the system: health care is not uniformly accessible, hospitals are inefficient, private practitioners are pushcart vendors in an age of supermarkets, and health care is really a nonsystem. Unfortunately, there is some truth to all of these charges. And psychiatry gets only faint praise for being one of the first specialities to advocate, to plan, and to strive to make mental health services more uniformly accessible.

Faced by the financial crunch, third-party payers have tried to justify reductions in benefits for mental health services by citing spectacular examples of dubious practice. There is, for example, the widely publicized claim submitted for four-times-a-week individual psychotherapy to a four-month old infant suffering from an adjustment reaction of infancy. CHAMPUS has been criticized [5] for paying claims for unproven treatment modalities rendered by substandard facilities. Such stories play on the public's irrational fears about the nature of mental illness and their suspicion of practitioners in this occult field. Without question, abuses should be prevented but these occasional instances of inappropriate treatment hardly contribute significantly to the cost of mental health care.

Accountability is being demanded from all providers because of the escalation in the cost of health care, greater reliance on public tax dollars, and skepticism concerning the reliability of professionals. The Social Security Amendments of 1972 (Public Law 92–603) call for professional standards review organizations. New utilization review regulations from the Department of Health, Education and Welfare now require review of hospital admissions within twenty-four hours to verify medical necessity, establishment of criteria for length of hospital stay, review of extended care, and on-going medical care evaluation studies. In the short run, such efforts are directed toward cost reduction by elimination of overutilization of services. For the long run, they are designed to make sweeping changes in the health care system.

In ten years, we have shifted 180° from the prohibitions in Medicare [6] against any ". . . federal officer or employee to exercise any supervision or control over the practice of medicine or the manner in which medical services are provided. . . ." Now, virtually all proposals for national health insurance legislation contain provisions that give the payer of services the authority and the means to use the financing mechanisms as an instrument to influence medical practice and to modify the health care system. Indeed, the Congress is likely to oppose any legislation that is not designed to make changes in the delivery system.

Medicare contains some instructive illustrations of the techniques that can be used: standard setting preferential coverage for certain providers, selective structuring of the benefits, to mention a few. For example, a psychiatric hospital to be eligible for Medicare must be accredited by the Joint Commission on the Accreditation of Hospitals or, at least, meet equivalent requirements. When Medicare made JCAH accreditation financially advantageous, there was a striking increase in the number of psychiatric hospitals that sought such accreditation. And hospitals are now rushing to meet the new utilization review requirements. This is not to suggest that it is bad to use the funding mechanism to upgrade standards; rather it is cited to illustrate how such a technique can be utilized.

Medicare applied a 190-day lifetime limit to treatment in psychiatric hospitals but not in general hospitals. Medicaid could be utilized in the psychiatric hospital only for patients over the age of 65 but was available for all patients, regardless of age, receiving psychiatric care in general hospitals. A departmental task force of the Social Security Administration, the Social Rehabilitation Service, and the Health Services and Mental Health Administration in studying the impact of these provisions [7], reported:

> Of all federal expenditures for hospital care, some eighteen percent went to psychiatric hospitals annually between 1962–1965; it had dropped to eight percent in 1968. In brief, federal funds for hospital care through Medicare and Medicaid has been directed largely and increasingly to general hospitals and only to a relatively small extent to psychiatric hospitals.

Under the Medicare supplementary medical insurance program covering physicians services, severe restrictions were and still are imposed on outpatient psychiatric treatment of mental illness. As a consequence [8] only two-tenths of 1 percent of those patients enrolled under Part B of Medicare utilized outpatient psychiatric services at a total reimbursement of only $2.1 million (after co-insurance payment), which was only three-tenths of 1 percent of the total expenditures under the supplementary medical insurance program. This low utilization for outpatient psychiatric services was in sharp contrast to steadily rising expenditures for other outpatient medical services.

Most efforts to change the system will likely be perceived only dimly by the psychiatric practitioner. The professional is far more attuned to procedures employed to monitor and control the treatment of individual patients. Such intrusions into the therapeutic relationship are interpreted as lack of trust and doubt of competence. Confidentiality is threatened. The review process itself is time-consuming, costly, and frustrating. And it is really hell when claims for payment are denied.

Nevertheless, like it or not, we are caught in an inexorable process: adequate health care has been declared the right of every person; making good on this commitment has proven enormously expensive; better organization, improved management, and tight control of the system are deemed essential; leadership and responsibility in matters of health are shifting from the health professions to government, private insurance, and the consumers. Accountability to patient and to peers is no longer judged enough; we are being challenged to document and convince skeptics of the need for services and their value to patients.

Psychiatric treatment is particularly vulnerable to challenge because of inherent difficulties in evaluation and outcome studies. Criteria for medical necessity, norms for predicting length of treatment, objective measures of outcome have just not been developed. Lacking such standards, many third-party payers exclude or arbitrarily limit psychiatric benefits. Evelyn Myers [9] reported:

> Many insurance programs do not cover mental illness, so only about 65 percent have in-hospital psychiatric benefits; only 55 percent have psychiatric in-hospital physician visits covered, and only about 30 percent have outpatient psychiatric coverage.

This approach is appealing because it requires little review, avoids legal challenge, and cuts costs.

For example, in a given year about 1 percent of subscribers to an insurance plan might seek outpatient psychiatric treatment. If the dollar amount is set as low as $400 per year (which has been done in some national plans), reasonably accurate forecasts of liability can be made and on the basis of experience, adjusted year by year. But such low limits will foster band-aid psychiatry and block innovation that could provide the data to support more definitive treatment approaches. This is the case under Medicare where the miniscule benefits for outpatient psychiatric treatment have reinforced institutionalization of the elderly and discouraged the development of active treatment in the community.

Another approach to cost containment is exemplified by what happened in the Federal Employees Health Benefit Plan in recent years. As the expense of health care escalated, the carriers sought to control costs through claims review. For psychiatrists working in hospitals such as myself this became a nightmare. More and more clinical information was required until complete records were demanded. Nonphysician reviewers screened these reports to determine whether the treatment was medically necessary, if the level of care was appropriate, if the services met acceptable standards, and if the treatment was covered by the contract. Claims questioned by nonphysician reviewers were referred to a physician for the determination of whether payment should be made. It has been acknowledged, however, that some programs just didn't have enough physician time available and few had psychiatric consultants available to make specialized clinical judgments.

Furthermore, denials of payment for psychiatric treatment based solely on chart reviews are open to serious question. Clinicians don't write progress notes and medical orders to satisfy claims review by third-party payers. Medical records have been designed to facilitate a patient's current treatment and to serve as a source of information should it be needed at some later time. So much for the technique of claims review, let's look at what actually happened.

In 1972 when a deficit as high as $60 million was predicted in the federal employees' program [10] denials of psychiatric claims increased sharply. Many denials were retroactive making patients liable for large medical bills. Few could risk an appeal because the financial obligation would continue to mount with no certainty that their insurance would pay.

Nevertheless, hospitals and patients began to fight against these denials. For example, my own experience was that during 1972–73 our hospital had 27 denials based on claims review and succeeded in reversing only eight although some ten appeals are still slowly working their way through the courts at great expense to the patients. With no fundamental change in treatment philosophy, during 1974–75 we had only eight denials, got seven reversals, leaving only one denied claim!

The widespread denial of claims was effective in reducing costs, but the feedback control was at best confusing. For example, claims were denied for "milieu therapy" because of specific exclusions in the contract [11] for this treatment modality. But what did the phrase mean? What was the intent of the exclusion? Was milieu therapy a euphemism for custodial care? Hardly, when denials for milieu therapy were made in acute psychiatric problems getting active treatment under individual treatment plans. This was all quite bewildering until a set of guidelines [12] prepared by a psychiatric consultant for claims reviewers leaked out.

The fifty pages of single-spaced guidelines [13] were in essence the psychiatric textbook for nonphysician claims reviewers. They contain such remarkable opinions as: "Psychiatry does not have the definitive structure of the medical sciences. It is composed of multiple philosophical disciplines with little agreement on methods of practice and a diffusion of contentious theories on the etiology and treatment of mental condition." Referring to treatment, they state: "The major groups and those most commonly associated with acute hospital care include medical, social, behavioral and psycho-biological schools of thought. Among a vast array of others are the analytic, transactional, transcendental, humanistic approaches to emotional problems."

The consultant [14] warns, "The current social environment of subsidy expectation has tended to place health care financing agents in the position of being viewed by both public and providers as automatic fiscal processing units. They therefore become the focus of more negative reactions, in the event of a denial, than would otherwise occur."

"Milieu therapy," which is excluded under the contract is described [15] as "training the person in the use of social skills" through the "hospital structure itself, the ward personnel, individual psychotherapy, group therapy, occupational therapy, psychodrama, relaxation groups, music therapy, and minor medication administration. Ancillary services include pool, volley ball, tennis, dancing, trips to nearby points of interest, hayrides, excursions to the beach, etc."

The preferred approach, medical psychiatry [16]: "is depicted in charts by a significant severity of illness, the use of principal therapeutic modalities such as major tranquilizers in relatively high dosage, convulsive therapy, insulin treatment, and intensive application of these. Group therapy, and recreational therapy are provided under general ward 'milieu' management, but these are not accentuated as primary methods of intervention." Additional guides used to judge whether claims should be paid describe a hierarchy in which the major modalities are limited to psychosurgery, insulin therapy, convulsive therapy, and major drug therapy. All other therapeutic approaches are classified as either adjunctive or ancillary.

It is bad enough that hundreds, perhaps thousands, of patients had their treatment interrupted by denial based on such a treatment philosophy. Consider the impact a claims review system could have on the future of psychiatry. Think of what could happen if these standards were adopted by NHI; only those hospitals and psychiatrists that were willing to accommodate to this new "school" of psychiatry would survive. It is alarming that these standards were open neither to public scrutiny nor scientific appraisal.

Still another system to monitor and control the Medicare and Medicaid programs, established by the Social Security amendments of 1972 [17], authorizes professional standards review organizations (PSROs) to assume the responsibility for utilization review and medical care evaluation. Let me emphasize that the legislation "authorizes," it does not require the establishment of PSROs. If physicians fail to establish a PSRO that meets federal regulations, the review process will be taken over by the Department of Health, Education and Welfare. Some physicians have objected and say they will not participate in PSROs. Such protests cause me to recall Senator Bennett's admonition to a physician testifying before the House Ways and Means Committee. When the physician threatened that doctors would *not* participate in PSROs, Senator Bennet, in effect, warned that doctors would have to realize that they were being given their last chance.

While PSROs have been stalled in the tedious struggle to meet complex and ambiguous requirements DHEW has established new requirements for utilization review that must be met by July 1, 1975. It must be assumed that these new regulations will be the basis for the review procedures expected from PSROs. These standards will undoubtedly be expanded to outpatient services and will be applied to any new federal health care legislation especially national health insurance. There is even some reason to think that private carriers might elect to accept findings by PSROs and qualified utilization review plans instead of, or at least in conjunction with, their own claims review.

The stated objectives for the new DHEW utilization review requirements include both high quality patient care as well as effective and efficient utilization of health facilities and services. The emphasis is, however, on cost containment. To qualify, a plan must include timely review of the medical necessity of admissions, extended stays, and professional services rendered. Key elements are an admissions review accomplished within the first twenty-four hours to assess the medical necessity of the patient's admission to the hospital in accordance with criteria previously developed by the medical staff. An initial extended-stay review date must be assigned in accordance with statistical norms for comparable patients. Authorization for a patient to stay beyond that date may be granted only if criteria previously established by the medical staff for continued stay are met. Medical care evaluation studies to examine the care rendered must be performed to promote the most effective and efficient use of available health resources consistent with patient needs and professionally recognized standards of health care.

Much of the review activity can be conducted by nonphysician patient review coordinators backed up by physician advisors. It is explicitly stated that a physician or nonphysician cannot participate in the review of any case in which he has been professionally involved. It is hard to believe that confidence and trust were once conveyed by the expression, "that's just what the doctor ordered."

The PSRO approach is often erroneously equated with peer review. Peer review is the traditional medical approach through which members of a profession assume responsibility for setting standards, reviewing practices, and maintaining ethical principles. By peer review, a profession exercises self-regulation and demonstrates it is worthy of the trust and sanctions accorded by society. PSROs are bureaucratic inventions that contain some elements of peer review but only within the constraints of several hundred explicit requirements contained in the new utilization review guidelines. Obviously DHEW does not consider traditional peer review adequate to monitor our increasingly complicated health care system.

Effective utilization review, regardless of who does it, is a formidable undertaking. Adequate techniques have not been developed for any branch of medicine, but in psychiatry the problems are especially difficult. Uniform criteria are not available to judge the need for hospitalization, to assess specific treatments, to determine length of hospital stay. Many diagnoses lack objective criteria, and goals of treatment may differ. Much of the statistical information now available has come from psychiatric units of general hospitals and is therefore not applicable for all facilities.

Despite these obstacles, considerable progress has been made. An APA Ad Hoc Committee on PSRO developed and published [19] in January 1974 model criteria sets for ten major groupings of psychiatric conditions that encompass 75 percent of hospitalized patients. These are being further refined by a Task Force for publication in the AMA Compendium [20], "Model Sets of Criteria for Screening the Appropriateness, Necessity and Quality of Medical Services in Hospitals." The criteria sets contain guidelines: to justify admission; to assess the adequacy of history, special examinations, lab studies, and special diagnostic studies; to evaluate the treatment plan including medications and special treatments. Using these guidelines, a non-physician can do an initial screen by selecting for physician review those charts not fulfilling the criteria. Only the most difficult questions need be studied by a peer review committee for decision and to further develop and refine the criteria.

To foster better collaboration, the APA Commission on Standards of Practice and Third Party Payment, at a March 1975 meeting [21], brought together representatives from major public and private health insurance programs with representatives from APA District Branch peer review committees from Illinois, District of Columbia, New York, Massachusetts, California, and Louisiana. These peer review committees reported on several years of successful experience reviewing questioned cases. The committees, on their own initiative, have variously engaged in studies of utilization, setting standards for specific treatment modalities, sponsoring legislation, and even developing agreements for binding arbitration. All have been able to protect confidentiality while achieving working relationships with the local carriers. Mr. H. G. Pearce, senior vice president, Blue Cross Association, indicated that the progress reported at this meeting [22] was the most impressive in some 25 years of contacts with provider groups. He looked forward to a time when all areas of the country had such peer review committees functioning.

To better understand the implications of review procedures on the future of the mental health delivery system, let me outline schematically the steps involved in the payment process. A patient seeks help, a practitioner or an institution provides a service; a claim is submitted to a third-party payer; the claim is either paid or it is not. This last step establishes a crucial feedback in the system.

So long as all claims are paid, the providers will continue to render services using their best professional judgment. Denials, on the other hand, introduce a whole new set of circumstances. Third-party payments must be made if claims are within the covered benefits of legislation, regulation, contract, or combination of these. Therefore, denials can be made only after all obligations to subscribers have been met. Payment can be withheld if the recipient of the service is not eligible; if the service is not covered; if the provider does not meet established standards; if the quantity of services exceeds some top limit. Assuming the service meets all of these tests it can still be denied if it is not medically necessary, if the quality of the service is inadequate, if the service is inefficiently carried out, if the duration of the service is too long. Obviously such denials based on the assessment of the services deserve special attention because difficult clinical judgments are required.

This complex process can be eliminated by tight constraints on the benefits. Detailed clinical reviews are made superfluous because the financial impact is kept at a low level. This approach has been extensively applied to outpatient psychiatric benefits. Evelyn Myers has noted that only about 30 percent of insurance programs have outpatient psychiatric coverage and even in that 30 percent it is common to have higher deductibles and higher coinsurance requirements.

When the scope and quantity of benefits are expanded, third-party payers are under greater obligation to review the services to assure that subscribers are getting appropriate treatment at a reasonable cost. If clinical reviews are conducted by the third party-payer, there are several consequences: clinical judgments will be susceptible to financial pressures; third-party payers seldom have enough clinicians to do adequate reviews; the criteria for the reviews are established by the payers and not the providers; the criteria are not open to public scrutiny; the findings of these reviews may lead the third-party payer to change the basic contract agreements under which treatment is provided. In short, claims review by the third-party payer is effective in achieving fiscal control but does little to improve the health care system.

If the providers of care are made a part of the review system, the consequences will be quite different. Admittedly, the fiscal control may not be as strong in the short run, although it could be more effective in the long run. The providers of care have the specialized professional competence needed for clinical reviews; criteria would be established by peers; findings could be more open to public scrutiny; professional organizations can apply stronger sanctions against abuses; findings can be used to improve all aspects of this system, including training, continuing education, and specialty certification. Providers would participate in the tough decisions needed for equitable allocation of resources to achieve adequate health care for all.

Recent developments in the CHAMPUS program, under which payment for medical services is made for dependents of military personnel, offers an instructive case study of these issues. In June 1974, when the program came under heavy congressional attack because of cost overruns, severe and arbitrary cutbacks [23] were announced. These cutbacks were rescinded in response to a storm of protest from military personnel and many psychiatric organizations. It emerged that CHAMPUS had done little monitoring of clinical services; payments had been made to substandard facilities for useless treatments. When the simple approach of cutting benefits proved politically unacceptable CHAMPUS officials sought assistance from the American Psychiatric Association [24]. The APA was able to offer immediate guidance for some of the problems and made a commitment to participate in attempts to establish better review mechanisms. Simultaneously, CHAMPUS, in collaboration with the National Institute of Mental Health, undertook a detailed professional review of mental health services [25] being rendered to children and adolescents in residential settings. Preliminary findings of this study suggest that mental health professionals can help administrators to utilize their resources more effectively. There are strong indications that a better understanding of the problems will lead psychiatrists to work through their professional organizations to improve clinical services.

Another encouraging collaboration began with the previously mentioned March meeting [26] when the APA Commission on Standards of Practice brought together third-party payers and APA peer review groups. At that meeting, Blue Cross shared guidelines being prepared for their claims reviewers. The proposed criteria for claims review have been circulated by the Commission to all peer review committees for criticism and recommendations [27]. Responses by peer review committees have been prompt and informative. The goal is a set of review criteria that is acceptable both to the third party payer and to the affected providers. It has already served as a stimulus to District Branch peer review groups. This could lighten the claims review burden carried by Blue Cross if they will accept findings by District Branch peer review committees.

Projects such as these involve a great deal of time and effort; and this is only the beginning. Some will protest that health professionals should be spared from such chores so they can spend their valuable time taking care of sick patients. But if we spend all our time taking care of patients and let others make critical administrative decisions, our patients will likely be sacrificed in the struggle against rising costs. We will lose any remaining opportunity for self determination over the practice of our profession.

Clearly no individual practitioner can stem the tide, though it is gratifying to see increasing numbers eager to help. Leadership by professional organizations with support from all members is required. Escalating costs and the shortage of health care resources make financial controls inevitable. If professionals are excluded from the control process, fiscal considerations will take precedence. Only the active participation of psychiatrists can assure high quality care and achieve effective and efficient use of resources.

Time is running out but there still seems to be a reasonable chance that psychiatrists can demonstrate to the consumer, private carriers, and government that peer review is the most effective way to achieve accountability and quality care.

## NOTES TO CHAPTER FOUR

1. Social Security Administration, *Bulletin*, January 1, 1974, (Washington, D.C.) Vol. 37, No. 1.

2. National Institute of Mental Health, *Insurance for Mental Health: Trends in the Delivery and Financing of Mental Illness Services in the United States*, 1974.

3. National Institute of Mental Health, *Insurance for Mental Health: Trends in the Delivery and Financing of Mental Illness Services in the United States*, 1974, p. 10.

4. National Institute of Mental Health, *Insurance for Mental Health: Trends in the Delivery and Financing of Mental Illness Services in the United States*, 1974, p. 11.

5. United States House of Representatives, Ninety-third Congress, *CHAMPUS and Military Health Care*, Report of Subcommittee No. 2 of the Committee on the Armed Forces (Washington, D.C.: U.S. Government Printing Office) December 1974.

6. U.S. Senate and House of Representatives, *Public Law 89–97, 89th Congress*, "Social Security Amendments of 1965," (Washington, D.C.: U.S. Government Printing Office) July 1965.

7. DHEW, SSA, Office of Research and Statistics, Research Report No. 37, *Financing Mental Health Care under Medicare and Medicaid*, (Washington, D.C.) 1971.

8. DHEW, SSA, Office of Research and Statistics, Research Report No. 37, *Financing Mental Health Care under Medicare and Medicaid*, (Washington, D.C.) 1971.

9. Myers, Evelyn, "National Health Insurance and Psychiatric Care: Prospects and Problems," PSYCHIATRIC ANNALS, (New York) January 1974.

10. American Psychiatric Association, *Psychiatric News*, "Blue Cross Claim Denials Spur Opposition, Probe," by Charles Hite (Washington, D.C.) April 17, 1974.

11. U.S. Civil Service Commission Bureau of Retirement, Insurance and Occupational Health, *Government Wide Service Benefit Plan 1975—The Blue Cross and Blue Shield Federal Employee Program* (As revised January 1, 1975) (Washington, D.C.).

12. Blue Cross/Blue Shield Federal Employees Program, *Claims Administration of Nervous and Mental Benefits* (Guidelines for Claims Review).

13. Same as 12, above.

14. Same as 12, above.

15. Same as 12, above.

16. Same as 12, above.

17. U.S. Senate and House of Representatives, *Public Law 92–603*, "Social Security Amendments of 1972," (Washington, D.C.: U.S. Government Printing Office), October 30, 1972.

18. Testimony before the Senate Finance Committee, February 7, 1971.

19. American Psychiatric Association (Washington, D.C.) *Model Criteria Sets*, Ad Hoc Committee on PSRO, January 1974.

20. American Medical Association, *Model Screening Criteria to Assist Professional Standards Review Organizations*, published in draft form, May 1975, under contract with HEW.

21. American Psychiatric Association, (Washington, D.C.) *Minutes of the Meeting of the Commission on Standards of Practice and Third Party Payers*, February 28–March 1, 1975.

22. Same as 21.

23. U.S. Department of Defense (Washington, D.C.) Memorandum dated June 7, 1974, signed by the Deputy Assistant Secretary of Defense.

24. American Psychiatric Association (Washington, D.C.) *Minutes of the Meeting of the Commission on Standards of Practice and Third Party Payers*, August 13, 1974.

25. National Institutes of Mental Health, *The Select Committee of Psychiatric Care and Evaluation (SCOPSE)*, chaired by Dana Prugh, M.D., DOD–NIMH Interagency Agreement, October 23, 1974.

26. Same as 21, above.

27. American Psychiatric Association (Washington, D.C.) *Minutes of the Meeting of the Committee on Peer Review*, October 1975, and correspondence.

Chapter Five

# Accountability in Psychiatric Practice: PSRO and Utilization Review

*Scott H. Nelson\**

Accountability is a word that is increasingly used in today's world, particularly in the health field. Essentially, it means being able to justify what we do, how we do it, and what it costs. Accountability is not a new concept to the field of business, for without it, a business could not succeed. However, the application of systems of accountability, which are being asked of us today, is relatively new to the practice of medicine.

In psychiatry, our task in becoming accountable is particularly difficult. This is because much of what we do in psychiatry is not demonstrable in as objective, scientific ways as is what is done by some other branches of medicine. For example, we psychiatrists may differ about the diagnosis for a given patient; even when there is agreement on diagnosis, we may disagree on the modality of treatment that is most appropriate. Unlike appendicitis or peneumonia, the outcome of many modalities of treatment in psychiatry are not easy to demonstrate, especially in short periods of time. Rather, changes are often subtle, difficult to measure, and occur over long periods of time. For these reasons, studies that attempt to measure

*Scott H. Nelson, M.D., is Director of the Office of Program Planning and Evaluation of the Alcohol, Drug Abuse, and Mental Health Administration, Department of HEW.

Dr. Nelson received his M.D. and M.P.H. from Harvard University and took his training in psychiatry at the Massachusetts Mental Health Center. He has served as Principal Mental Health Officer and Principal Medical Officer for the Job Corps, and is the author of numerous publications in mental health and health research, practice and administration.

Note: The opinions expressed in this paper are those of the author, and do not necessarily reflect those of the Alcohol, Drug Abuse, and Mental Health Administration, the Department of Health, Education and Welfare, or the U.S. Public Health Service.

outcome in the field of psychiatry often are complex, expensive, and frequently inconclusive.

Society, courts, insurance companies, and others are asking the field of psychiatry to overcome these difficulties, many of which are inherent in the practice of psychiatry and increasingly to justify diagnosis and treatment provided, particularly when it is being financed by public dollars. This is a challenge of enormous magnitude—of a magnitude perhaps greater than that faced by any other specialty of medicine. It is also a challenge that psychiatrists and the other mental health professions as well must meet successfully in order to increase the likelihood of continuing to participate in third-party reimbursement for delivery of health services to people in need, and certainly to be able to justify expanded coverage.

Why has the concept of accountability been introduced in the practice of medicine, and particularly in psychiatry, in the recent past? A number of answers can be provided to this question.

First, accountability practices give greater assurance that the quality of care provided is adequate. In our period of rapid growth as a profession over the last quarter-century, we have encouraged the public to be aware of mental disorder and its signs and symptoms. Much of the public has become more aware; they also are aware of the different modalities that can be provided for treatment of psychiatric disorder and are more sophisticated about what constitutes high quality care for their families. In part, this increased sophistication has led to consumers' demands on physicians for provision of adequate quality of care.

In addition, the days in which a physician is assumed automatically to be a humanitarian helper of good will are over. Malpractice insurance rates are growing exponentially. As you know, in several states, insurance companies are reluctant to insure physicians at all for provision of medical care.

Furthermore, unfortunately, those psychiatrists and other mental health professionals who do not practice competently or ethically tend to tarnish the image of the entire field. This is an insidious but extremely important factor in the current call for increased accountability. Recall, for example, the psychiatrist in New York who was convicted of having sex with his patient and was assessed damages of $350,000 in March of this year [1]. Consider the findings of Senator Jackson's Committee that discovered that emotionally disturbed children were treated with inhumane procedures in some residential treatment facilities for children. Some children were held captive in chains and were forced to dig their own graves as part of "treatment" [2].

Unfortunately, such episodes are remembered not only by the public-at-large but also by insurance companies, many of which provide benefits for psychiatric and other mental health professional care. In the summer of 1974, the concern of insurance companies about psychiatric care in general rose to a peak. At that time, the CHAMPUS program (Civilian Health and Medical Program of the Uniformed Services), which serves the dependent population of the Armed Forces, announced a cut back of their benefits for mental health care to 120 inpatient days and 40 outpatient visits from previously unlimited reimbursement. At the same time, the federal employees' Blue Cross–Blue Shield program also indicated that it was about to reduce its unlimited benefit package. In initial discussions, it appeared that the reasons for this were primarily those relating to the rate of rise of the percentage of cost attributable to mental disorder in the federal Blue Cross–Blue Shield plan. However, closer examination and discussion with Blue Cross–Blue Shield officials indicated that there were other reasons as well. For example, reviewers of claims submitted for psychiatric benefits were skeptical that treatment was effective. Some patients had been in treatment for several years without any demonstrable effect. Claims reviewers felt that some treatment claims were inappropriate. For example, one claim was cited in which a four-month old child was billed for individual psychotherapy, while his parents were billed separately as well.

Although CHAMPUS reversed its cutbacks and the Blue Cross–Blue Shield federal program did not cut back its benefits last year, the next largest federal employees' plan (Aetna) did make outpatient cutbacks to 20 visits in the private setting and 40 visits in a community mental health center. Such actions by insurance companies are not uncommon in today's economy, where dollars are scarce and choices among alternatives must be made. However, the choices just described result only in part from concern with costs. They also show a concern that psychiatry as a field lacks scientific rigor with regard to diagnosis, and the selection of treatment modality. They reflect the difficulty that psychiatry has had in showing effectiveness of many modalities of treatment. They sometimes also demonstrate the bias and stigma that has frequently been attached to those who are emotionally disturbed or who have problems with alcoholism and drug abuse, and to those programs and institutions that treat such individuals.

But perhaps even more disturbing is the fact that visit limits and fiscal cutbacks often reflect the simple fact that psychiatry and the other mental health professions have not been concerned enough about these perceptions of our field. We have not been concerned enough with the fact that a substantial number of consumers and third-party payers consider mental health treatment to be unnecessary, or designed largely to fill the coffers of practitioners. We have not taken action to require psychiatrists to conform to any standards of competent psychiatric practice. We in the field of psychiatry have not, on our own, sufficiently taken on policies and procedures of assuring accountability to our own profession, to third-party payers, and to the public we serve.

## THE MEANING OF ACCOUNTABILITY

A variety of existing laws, policies, and procedures define accountability in an operational sense for the medical community, including psychiatry. The major piece of legislation is the Professional Standards Review Organization legislation that was passed as part of the Social Security amendments of 1972 (Public Law 92–603). The major procedures, however, that have been used to assure accountability in the medical field have been those of utilization review, medical audit (or Medical Care Evaluation Studies—MCES), and program evaluation. Let me take a moment to define each of these terms.

### Utilization Review

Utilization review is a process by which the care for an individual patient is reviewed with regard to the appropriateness of care. This review may occur *before* the care is delivered (prospective review), *during* the period that the care is being delivered (concurrent review), or *after* the care is delivered (retrospective review). In order to determine whether or not treatment is appropriate, standards must be developed for specific aspects of care. If the care is to be provided in a hospital setting, these would include for each condition a justification for admission, anticipated length of stay, treatment modalities to be utilized, discharge plan, and other pertinent aspects. Peer review is a kind of utilization review in which standards and procedures accepted by the peer profession are applied to the review process.

The purposes of utilization review may be limited to assuring the patient receives the most appropriate kind of care. On the other hand, other goals may also be legitimate in a utilization review program. For example, a utilization review procedure may want to assure that treatment is not excessive, thereby reducing costs to a more appropriate level. This is particularly important in programs that are working on a fixed, limited budget. Utilization review may also be used to introduce standards that would assure higher quality of care than the minimum required.

### Medical Audit

The medical audit function is known as Medical Care Evaluation Studies in the PSRO program. Medical audit is a methodology that provides certain patterns of utilization and care by longitudinal study over a period of time. For example, the utilization of a given psychiatric service by a specific patient could be assessed and inappropriate use could be addressed. The prescribing patterns of physicians or the use of a given treatment modality for specific psychiatric diagnoses could be examined. Systematic medical audit procedures potentially can be of great use in determining where problems exist in the service delivery system and can suggest ways of resolving these problems to administrators. They also can identify areas in which continuing education for practitioners may be indicated. However, particular care needs to be paid to issues of confidentiality for both patient and practitioner.

### Program Evaluation

Program evaluation refers to the process by which an organized system of care is assessed with regard to its success or failure in meeting certain specified objectives. The objectives should be explicit and feasible—that is, the process of evaluation should be able to determine whether or not the objectives were achieved.

Medical audit procedures may often be utilized to evaluate part of a program of psychiatric care. However, program evaluation usually extends beyond the limits of medical audit to other aspects of the program, such as assuring standards of humane treatment of patients and protection of confidentiality and patients' rights.

Having tried to convey some background and definitions, I'd like to describe briefly some examples of utilization review systems that are already or soon will be in operation, for those of you who are not familiar with utilization review as a procedure. These are the systems at the Peninsula Community Mental Health Center in San Mateo, California, the utilization review process as it is envisioned under Professional Standards Review Organizations, and some specific activities underway at the National Institute of Mental Health.

## PENINSULA COMMUNITY MENTAL HEALTH CENTER

The Peninsula Community Mental Health Center is located in a general hospital in Burlingame, California, and serves the population of San Mateo County, south of San Francisco. The Center provides service delivery almost exclusively through private practitioners, most of whom are psychiatrists. Like many community mental health centers, Peninsula has been responsible for serving a total catchment area and providing unlimited service, while its budget is limited. In 1969, the Center's administration became highly concerned that financial expenditures were exceeding the limited Medicaid and Short Doyle budgets for inpatient and outpatient services. At that time, a peer review system was established for review of all cases to be reimbursed under the Short Doyle or Medicaid program.

Four peer review committees exist at the Center: (1) a Child Committee, (2) an Adult Outpatient Committee, (3) an Adult Inpatient Committee and (4) a Partial Hospitalization Committee. Practitioners who wish to treat a patient longer than six outpatient visits or who hospitalize their Short Doyle or Medicaid patients must present the case of the patient to the appropriate Peer Review Committee.

Discussions then are held on the type and amount of treatment that will be necessary and the committee makes a decision about the number of sessions that can be authorized for the therapist to see the patient. After the authorized number of sessions has elapsed, the case is usually reviewed again.

As one might imagine, a good deal of constructive tension is created by this process—that is, between the need to operate within a limited budget and the need to deliver treatment that is compatible with the practitioner's training and experience and is appropriate for the patient's needs. This is usually worked out on an individual basis rather than by the committee's attempting to adhere to specified criteria and standards. About two-thirds of the presenting practitioners feel that the committees maintained an appropriate balance between cost and quality considerations.

The practitioners generally support the peer review system. In a study conducted by the Center, participants in the peer review process felt that the system had assisted in both cost control (90 percent) and to a lesser extent in improving quality of care (80 percent). Over 90 percent felt that the system provided a positive educational experience [3]. The majority of practitioners felt that it did not affect their treatment relationship either positively or negatively. However, very few felt that their review of treatment for Short Doyle and Medicaid patients affected how they set goals or treated other patients. Those who presented more frequently tended to feel more positively about the peer review experience than those who presented less.

Also related to the practitioners' support appears to be the fact that the community mental health center serves as a major resource for referrals of patients and the fact that the peer review sessions serve as a mechanism for obtaining case consultation and continuing education. Poor quality of care is usually addressed by asking practitioners to re-present the patient in a relatively short period of time and by discussing the specifics of treatment more in detail.

Over the past three years, the peer review process has helped to keep the community mental health center within its Medicaid and Short Doyle budgets. However, during the current year there has been an overrun again, and the committees are now being encouraged to take a more strict stance with regard to their recommendations and decisions concerning treatment. It should be noted that while in this instance the mental health center must adapt its review procedures to budgetary circumstances, the question of whether or not utilization is appropriate, too little or even excessive is not able to be answered—a clear limitation both of the review system and a reflection of the state of our knowledge about the effectiveness of various treatment patterns and modalities.

## PROFESSIONAL STANDARDS REVIEW
## ORGANIZATIONS (PSRO)

Turning now to PSROs, Professional Standards Review Organizations are authorized under Section 249(f) of Public Law 92–603, the amendments to the Social Security legislation of 1972. This law basically provides for the review of care delivered to recipients of Medicare-Medicaid and Maternal and Child Health Services to be sure that they are medically necessary, meet professionally recognized standards, and are appropriately provided in the most economical sites by appropriate practitioners.

A PSRO is a locally based organization. When the PSRO program is fully implemented, there will be one PSRO for each of 203 designated geographic areas in the United States. Each PSRO will be responsible for developing standards of care for the most common conditions and for implementing a process by which exceptions to the standards can be reviewed. This process will apply equally to psychiatry as well as to the other medical specialties. At the present time, the review procedures will be utilized only for acute general hospital inpatient care. Requirements will gradually be implemented for assumption of review of long-term care and ambulatory service as well.

The American Psychiatric Association has been a leader in developing standards for the medical specialties in review of utilization of care. The APA's initial criteria sets were developed in January 1974 and have recently been revised to conform to the AMA's format for the development of PSRO standards [4].

How will the PSRO mechanism affect me as a practitioner? I can't answer that question specifically, but let me give you my impression of how it will work. Assuming that the PSRO is established, it will probably take the American Psychiatric Association's criteria sets and modify them to its own particular local needs and patterns of psychiatric practice. Once these have been agreed upon by the local PSRO, these will then be used by the PSRO review mechanism system. This system will typically be set up as follows: A nurse will be trained to review all charts submitted in conjunction with claims for Medicaid, Medicare, or Maternal and Child Health Service reimbursement. He or she will be fully familiar with the standards that have been established for the most common psychiatric conditions by the local PSRO. The nurse will then review each chart or a sample of charts for conformance with the standards that have been set. Those charts that meet the standards will be reimbursed with no further question except determining the answers to technical questions such as patient eligibility and entitlement to benefits. Those records that fall outside the standards, either because an unusual treatment was performed, or because inadequate documentation of what was done was submitted, will be set aside for further review. This would not necessarily indicate that the physician would not be reimbursed for this care, but only that the particular instance fell outside the normative standards set by the local PSRO. This exceptional case would then be reviewed by either the central PSRO for the designated area or by a utilization review panel of physicians which had been delegated the responsibility for review. This could be, in the example of a psychiatric patient, a group of physicians and/or psychiatrists working in the general hospital, or eventually even a multidisciplinary mental health professional committee. This group would review the chart and the other aspects of the case, consult the treating physician when necessary, and make a decision with regard to the case in question.

Using concurrent review procedures to evaluate need for admission and for continued stay, and medical care evaluation studies to determine patterns of care, the PSRO process has potential for bringing about some significant positive benefits to the field of psychiatry. It should help to identify practitioners who require additional training and/or education with regard to diagnosis and treatment. It also hopefully will protect the public and the psychiatric profession from incompetent practitioners.

Yet the PSRO process, and systems of accountability in general, will undoubtedly have their limitations as well. They probably will not help much in improving the organization of service delivery; to the extent that the mental health system reviews its care separately from the rest of the health system, opportunities for us to enlighten practitioners in other specialties to important factors in quality care and vice versa will be lost. One example of the desirability for this mutual educational experience is the clear need in the review process for physicians to be sufficiently sensitive to social factors, which are highly important factors in determining appropriate levels of care for many mental disorders and also for chronic medical conditions. The point is that accountability systems are not panaceas, but may play important roles in the upgrading and maintenance of high quality care.

## THE NIMH ROLE

While the locally based PSROs are developing, there are more urgent issues that relate to accountability in psychiatric practice that have required the immediate attention of the National Institute of Mental Health, in the Department of Health, Education and Welfare. As has been mentioned, there has been considerable concern expressed in the Congress in recent months regarding the nature of some of the residential treatment facilities for children that CHAMPUS was reimbursing for mental health services. The Department of Defense, which has responsibility for the CHAMPUS program, asked the NIMH for assistance in establishing a utilization and quality review program to address the quality of care in these residential treatment facilities initially and later possibly other mental health treatment programs as well.

Through the leadership of the NIMH, twenty teams, consisting of one child psychiatrist and one other mental health professional, are now reviewing cases of children who have been confined in a residential facility for more than 120 days. In addition, when there are repeated questions about the quality of services provided in a residential facility that is eligible for reimbursement under CHAMPUS, the teams will make a site visit to assure that quality care is being provided.

In response to the concern of insurance carriers in the Federal Employees' Health Benefit program, the NIMH is working with the Civil Service Commission and some of the major professional associations, including the American Psychiatric Association, to attempt to set up a utilization review process to assure that claims are appropriate.

Success or failure of these attempts to set up utilization review procedures within CHAMPUS and the federal employees' insurance program will attest to how effectively utilization review can be implemented in the mental health, drug abuse and alcoholism fields. This evidence will be important, not only for the continuing development of utilization and peer review systems and the PSRO program, but even more importantly to justify and improve mental health, drug abuse, and alcoholism benefit levels under national health insurance, where some form of utilization review certainly will be required.

## ADDITIONAL ISSUES
## RELATED TO ACCOUNTABILITY
## IN PSYCHIATRIC PRACTICE

We have talked a good deal about what accountability is and some examples of its application in psychiatric practice. But given difficulties in agreement on diagnosis, appropriate treatment, and measurement of outcome, and the concern of insurance carriers of third-party payers and the public about psychiatric practice, our achieving a system of effective and efficient accountability in a short period of time will indeed be a challenge.

Other, more specific issues will also confront psychiatrists as we attempt to develop and implement an effective system of accountability for our care of patients. For example, how can we interact most effectively with other mental health professional disciplines in the review of care? What should be the appropriate role of consumers in assuring accountability of psychiatric and other mental health practice?

Facing us in the future we will have the difficult task of developing standards for outpatient care, long-term care, partial hospitalization, and children's services. And all along the way, we must assure that the confidential relationship between the physician and patient as well as the patients' rights to privacy are protected. This is particularly important where a large program is being implemented and where large-scale data systems are being used. Such issues as what kind of information should be collected, what will be done with the information, and how it can be used towards improvement of the system without penalizing practitioners, patients, or the taxpayers unnecessarily are issues that will need to be considered.

One of the aspects of formal systems of accountability that produces most concern on the part of psychiatrists is whether or not accountability procedures will interfere with high quality care of patients. I think it is fair to say that it is likely that any process that scrutinizes on a routine basis the practice of mental health care will lead to some changes in the way in which care is delivered. For the most part, these changes will be positive ones—that is, they will assist the profession as a whole to practice more in accord with local standards of high quality and competence. Review procedures will also serve the function of case consultation and continuing education for psychiatrists.

On the other hand, there is legitimate concern that systems of accountability, particularly as they are newly developing, may impose arbitrary standards on practitioners, even though they are applied from within one's own profession. In addition, some are worried that innovative and new procedures for treatment would not be able to be used. There appear to be no easy answers to these problems; all of us, however, should keep a close watch on these and other identified potential difficulties in the developing process of accountability so that they can be dealt with early and effectively.

One common misconception about utilization review and medical audit programs is that they are designed to limit the amount of care that can be provided. This simply is not so. Limits on reimbursement are set through insurance carriers, state or other rate setting agencies, or will be established under a more global mechanism in the future such as national health insurance. Accountability systems are set up to assure that necessary and appropriate care is delivered. In the event that care is not necessary or is inappropriately delivered, as determined by peers, it is true that reimbursement may in some instances be denied. However, generally speaking, the focus is on educating practitioners in the hopes of improving their performance rather than on reducing their access to a financial reimbursement.

In addition, it should be made clear that the PSRO will not be able to tell physicians how they must practice. It cannot say that a hospitalized patient must be discharged, for example. It *can* tell a practitioner that it will no longer pay for a patient's care while that patient stays in the hospital. The physician then has to consult with the patient and make the judgment as to whether or not the patient needs to remain in the hospital at his or her own expense or whether the patient is psychiatrically well enough to be discharged.

It should be pointed out, however, that a relationship between limits on reimbursement for emotional problems and effective review of care does and should exist. This relationship, briefly summarized, is that if insurance carriers and health policy makers believe that effective review of necessary and appropriate care is being carried out, they may well be more willing to extend the limits of care which can be reimbursed. This is particularly important as national health insurance approaches. However, it also places the burden of responsibility for effective review of care squarely on us, the psychiatric profession.

One of the greatest concerns of psychiatrists is that systems of accountability may force us to change our traditional methods of practice. Such changes also may result from limits on financial reimnursement for service. The concern simply stated is that the limitations imposed by third-party carriers on numbers of service visits, and the requirements of accountability systems for service efficiency and effectiveness may not allow us as psychiatrists to use modalities such as long-term psychoanalytically oriented psychotherapy and psychoanalysis as frequently as before. Many practitioners feel that such changes in numbers of visits or treatment approach by definition can be equated with inferior quality care.

Unfortunately, this is where our internal professional disagreements about the most effective treatment modalities and our difficulties in measuring short- and long-term treatment outcomes become exceedingly important.

Where effectiveness data do not support it, longer-term treatment is going to be more difficult to justify in the current economic climate than shorter treatment. What would seem to be the eventual outcome is that either substantial outcome studies and controlled clinical trials that might (or might not) justify longer-term treatment must be done, or our profession must come to terms with changes in our approach to treatment. In the face of our increasing need to be responsive to financial limitations and accountability systems, and despite the optimism of D. H. Malan in his December 1973 article in the *Archives of General Psychiatry,* in which some problems demonstrating effectiveness of psychotherapy is described, some change in the nature of psychiatric practice seems to me to be most likely.

The issues here are complex ones. Let's take a hypothetical specific example of a couple who comes to a psychiatrist for treatment of a marital problem. What difference would there be between treatment that has no financial limitation on the number of sessions as opposed to a system that allows only 30 visits? Most of us believe that the expectations of patients are extremely important in treatment outcome. Could we say with certainty that the 30-visit limit necessarily reduces the quality of care the couple will receive? The 30-visit limitation certainly does force very specific expectations on both sides; but it also provides incentives for specific goals to be articulated and accomplished in the therapy.

Traditionally, the couple might be seen twice a week. But do we have data that indicates that this is a better pattern of treatment than say once a week or even twice a month? With a 30-visit limit, the process of treatment could go on for more than a year (which is the usual insurance benefit) with twice a month visits, while treatment would last less than four months with twice a week visits.

The problems are more serious, of course, for persons with more chronic mental disorders, but this example illustrates the problem we have in supporting our traditional assumptions about treatment with data. Clinical trials and outcome studies, as mentioned previously, are very sparse. In addition, they are exceedingly complex and expensive to design and conduct. Yet it is precisely these kinds of studies that are needed to justify the legitimacy of various patterns and modalities of treatment, and ultimately, financial reimbursement for the various forms of psychiatric practice. The most important end point for these endeavors is national health insurance, in which hopefully psychiatry and the other mental health professions will be full participants.

## SUMMARY AND CONCLUSION

In this chapter, I have attempted to outline the background related to the issues surrounding accountability in psychiatric practice. Definitions of accountability approaches, such as utilization review, medical audit, and program evaluation have been suggested, and some examples of utilization review from the Peninsula Community Mental Health Center, the PSRO program and the National Institute of Mental Health have been given. I have tried to highlight some of what I consider the major issues that are unresolved or need to be addressed with regard to accountability systems. These include development of standards for settings outside of the inpatient units of general hospital, concerns about confidentiality, and the need for improved data about the effectiveness of treatment patterns and modalities.

Of greatest concern to me, however, is our profession's relative unwillingness until recently to take on responsibility itself for becoming more accountable. Fortunately, there seems to be hope. There is increasing interest in psychiatry in clinical trial research and evaluation. Many APA district branches now have active ethics and peer review committees, and psychiatrists have begun to participate actively in many areas of the country in utilization review systems and PSROs. I cannot overemphasize the importance of continuing this momentum. In this day and age, we cannot afford in the psychiatric profession to bury our heads in the sand and allow the review of our care to be conducted solely by claims reviewers and others who are appropriately concerned with the economics of care and with accountability, but who have little knowledge of psychiatric practice. Rather, the leadership should come from us; accountability systems should be developed and maintained by those professionals who deliver the care, so that decisions can be made with our full input and participation. To the extent that we fail to be willing to take on this responsibility, this work will be done for us. And this would be unfortunate not only for us as psychiatrists, but most of all for the patients whom we serve.

## NOTES TO CHAPTER FIVE

1. Medical World News, May 5, 1975.

2. Hearings Before the Permanent Subcommittee on Investigation of the Committee on Government Operations, U.S. Senate, 93rd Congress, July 25 and 26, 1974.

3. Peninsula Hospital Community Mental Health Center, *Evaluation of a Prototype Psychiatric PSRO*, Final Report of Contract No. ADM–42–74–91, National Institute of Mental Health, September 1975.

4. American Psychiatric Association, *Model Criteria ScFs*, January 1974.

## REFERENCES

*American Journal of Psychiatry.* "Special Section: PSRO and Other Peer Review Mechanisms," Vol. 131. 1974.

Joint Commission on Mental Illness and Health. 1961. *Action for Mental Health,* Final Report of the Joint Commission on Mental Illness and Health. New York: Basic Books.

Malan, David H. 1973. "The Outcome Problem in Psychotherapy Research," *Archives of General Psychiatry* 29.

Newman, Donald E. 1974. "Peer Review, A California Model," *Psych. Annals* 4.

Tarter, Ralph E., Templer, Donald L., and Hardy, Charlotte. 1975. "Reliability of the Psychiatric Diagnosis," *Diseases of the Nervous System* 36.

# Chapter Six

# Third Party Payers: Current Status and Future Alternatives

*Robert J. Laur**

My contribution to this volume will arise from a portrayal of the current arrangements for financing mental health services and some speculation on what the future might hold. In the remarks that follow, I have deliberately said little about the inclusion of mental benefits in national health insurance or present governmental programs that support care of the mentally ill, since these are covered in other chapters. At the onset, I believe it would be helpful if I spent just a few moments in an attempt to clarify health insurance jargon, into which I am sure to slip as this chapter progresses.

The American enthusiasm for diversity is certainly apparent in our approach to the financing of health care. Commercial insurance companies have written health policies for a long time, often as companion business to life, accident, or liability insurance. Since the 1930s, not-for-profit Blue Cross and Blue Shield Plans have become major underwriters of care. In certain industries or communities, health and welfare plans of unions or employee organizations are a source of financing. And of course health maintenance organizations have been receiving considerable attention of late, although they are hardly a new phenomenon. All of these organizations, along with

*Robert J. Laur is Vice-President of the Blue Cross Association and the National Association of Blue Shield Plans, and Director of the Federal Employee Program of Blue Cross and Blue Shield.

Dr. Laur received his undergraduate and graduate degrees at the University of Minnesota where he taught in the program in Hospital Administration. He has been Assistant Professor in the Department of Community Health and Medical Practice at the University of Missouri School of Medicine and has held several government posts including Director of the Office of Policy, Development, and Planning, Office of the Assistant Secretary for Health Department of Health, Education, and Welfare.

many patients who pay their bills out-of-pocket, make up what is often termed the "private sector" of health care financing.

Public sector support for health care is perhaps even more complex, if that's possible. There are government-operated health systems such as Veterans Administration hospitals, the Indian Health Service, military health care facilities, and hospitals or other care programs sponsored by state or local governments. In addition, public financing of health care is accomplished through payments made on behalf of individuals who, by law, have an entitlement to financial support. Examples are the Medicare program of the Social Security Administration, Medicaid, which is a joint program of federal and state governments, and the CHAMPUS program for dependents and retirees of the military. Finally, public support for health care can come in the form of grants-in-aid for construction and operation of facilities, research and manpower development.

The term *third-party payer* is customarily used to describe financing arrangements where care is paid for on behalf of eligible individuals, whether they be employees covered under a collectively bargained health insurance plan, subscribers to health insurance policies, or persons entitled to coverage through a governmental program.

The types of coverage offered by third-party payers can be classified many ways. One way is to ask: "To whom does the third party make the payment—the individual or the provider of service? Payments made to individuals are called *indemnity payments*, because the third party is indemnifying the person for a payment he has already made to a provider of care. On the other hand, if the third party pays the provider directly on behalf of the subscriber, this is called a *service benefit*. This is the type of coverage commonly associated with Blue Cross and Blue Shield Plans or with health maintenance organizations.

Another classification of health insurance payments has to do with the concept of cost-sharing on behalf of the patient or subscriber. Some third-party payers offer *paid-in-full benefits*, meaning that the entire bill (for the services covered by the policy) will be paid. Paid-in-full benefits are most often found in connection with service benefit plans, since the third-party can negotiate directly with providers of care.

In contrast to paid-in-full benefits are those where the subscriber must pay an initial amount (a *deductible*) or share fractionally in the payment of the bill (*co-insurance*). These cost-sharing arrangements may be incorporated into a health insurance contract for many reasons. Large deductibles eliminate small costly claims and make possible low rates for rare, but potentially costly illnesses. These are the so-called "major medical" or "catastrophic" policies. Cost-sharing may also be used where the insurer feels the subscriber may abuse his coverage by seeking unnecessary care. Finally, there are instances where it is felt that the success of therapy depends upon some out-of-pocket expenditures by the patient.

With this brief explanation of terminology behind us, I would now like to examine the state of third-party financing for mental services. As I indicated earlier, the review of public programs will largely be left to other writers in this volume.

In recent years, a number of analyses have been made of the scope and form of health insurance coverage for mental health services [1]. At the risk of over-simplification, the conclusions of these studies would generally seem to be:

1. Until the 1960s, health insurance coverage for mental services was largely restricted to hospital inpatient care. Limitations on cover-age for hospital services of all kinds were common, but usually these were more restrictive for mental services.
2. During the 1960s, experimentation began with coverage of out-patient services, typically under major medical benefits rather than basic. Hospital benefits for all types of conditions broadened, and in general mental benefits for inpatient care were made compa-rable to surgical and medical benefits.
3. A significant proportion of total expenditures for mental health services continued to come from governmental sources, although emphasis shifted from support primarily of large mental hospitals to a more balanced support of hospitals, community mental health centers, and care in offices of private practitioners.
4. Accompanying these changes, and probably contributing to them, were changing public attitudes about mental illness. While mental health services still appear to be less positively accepted by the public than are those for physical illness, this stigmatization is no longer a major barrier to the provision or financing of mental care. Public and provider apathy may now be the attitudinal obstacle that must be overcome if mental health services are to become more widely accessible and affordable.

From the foregoing, I conclude that the feasibility of providing third-party coverage for mental health services has been well estab-lished—at least for such "traditional" services as inpatient hospital care and office care. The experience of the health benefits program that Blue Cross and Blue Shield Plans offer, on a nationwide basis, to employees of the federal government tends to support this conclusion. Since 1968, coverage has been provided on an equal basis for both mental and physical illnesses.

In 1974, approximately 5.5 million federal employees and their dependents were covered under the Blue Cross and Blue Shield program. Approximately 1 percent of the subscribers received at least one covered mental health service during the year. Mental benefits accounted for 7.2 percent of all benefit payments; $70 million out of a total of $979 million paid for all claims. It should be recognized that many claims for physical illness services in fact cover mental services and therefore claims data tend to understate the "true" level of mental services rendered and paid for.

Since 1968, there have been annual increases in the dollars spent for mental benefits per person enrolled in the federal employee program. For several years, benefit dollars per average covered population increased at a rate of about 20 percent each year. Then the rate of increase began to moderate in 1972 and 1973. Of course, some of this deceleration can be attributed to the price controls instituted under the Economic Stabilization Program, but the more moderate rate of increase seems to have continued into 1974. In that year, benefits per covered person for mental care increased 8.5 percent, compared to a 10.8 percent increase for all other types of care. This marked the first year since at least 1964 that mental benefit payments increased at a lower rate than did all other types of care.

To put our current experience in different terms, in 1974 we paid out $188.95 per covered person (in our high option plan, which 87 percent of our federal subscribers select). Of this amount, $13.73 went for mental benefits and the remaining $175.22 for all other types of care. In comparison, mental benefits per person in 1968 amounted to $6.06 out of total payments of $94.97.

Federal employees and the federal government have been willing thus far to pay the subscription rates necessary to support a broad service benefit plan, even when costs have been escalating so rapidly. This is not to say that this trend will continue, however. Indeed, we see clear indications that the climate is changing. In recent years, we have been unable to negotiate rates that will provide for prudent reserves for this program. Congressional scrutiny of rate increases has been intense and generally critical, with the suggestion being made that we should do even more to hold down prices charged by hospitals and doctors. Other health insurance carriers are experiencing similar difficulties, especially when their rates are subject to federal or state review, as is the case for most Blue Cross and Blue Shield Plans.

Adding to these difficulties, in the case of our federal employee program, is a contractual limitation on the amount of administrative expenses that we can charge. Although we still manage to return 95 cents of every premium dollar to our subscribers in benefits, we are finding that out-of-hospital benefits (especially those which are paid in full directly to providers) are considerably more costly to administer. And, of course, out-of-hospital benefits are the ones that have grown most dramatically as we have broadened our coverage.

From an overall perspective, it makes sense to provide coverage for ambulatory services if, in so doing, costly and unnecessary hospitalization expenses can be avoided. But to keep the administrative costs for ambulatory services down to a reasonable fraction of the benefit costs, it is clear that third-party payers and providers must develop more imaginative procedures and more cooperative relationships than we enjoy today.

This imperative is especially pressing in regard to coverage for mental health services, in my opinion, for the following reasons:

1. Compared to other types of services, there is less clarity and uniformity of terminology concerning mental diagnoses, treatment modalities and types of facilities providing care. Adjudicating claims under these conditions adds a considerable amount to carrier administrative expenses.
2. In common with other chronic illnesses, care for chronic mental conditions can extend over long time periods, and at considerable expense. To contain claims payments to medically necessary and contractually specified benefits in ambiguous areas, most insurers employ one or more of the following:
   a. Deductibles and/or co-insurance.
   b. Specific limits on the number of days of hospitalization or office visits that will be covered.
   c. Specific "inside" dollar limits on payments that will be made for certain types of services.
   d. Some form of utilization and quality review that validates the care rendered. In chronic illnesses, it is important that this validation be done on a concurrent or at least a frequent basis.
   e. If timely validation is not accomplished, the patient may be faced with denial of coverage for an expensive service after sizeable bills have accumulated.
   f. If subscribers and providers want coverages that are not arbitrarily limited, or do not require high cost-sharing provisions, then it is necessary that creditable, reliable and uniform utilization review processes be established. (For mental health services,

such processes are not widely available today. I believe their absence constitutes the single most important barrier to the extension of mental health coverage by third-party payers.)

What are the prospects for the future? To my regret, I personally find it difficult to be optimistic about the improvement of third-party payment for mental health services, at least for the next few years. And my pessimism extends to commercial insurance, government-supported programs such as Medicare or national health insurance, health maintenance organizations, and nonprofit plans such as Blue Cross and Blue Shield. This gloomy conclusion is a result of the following observations:

First, in 1974, as a result of a rather thorough review of our coverage for mental services, we concluded that we should increase our basic (paid-in-full) coverage by adding basic benefits for a specific number of out-of-hospital visits, and for day/night care. We proposed to reduce hospital coverage to 45 days (our average length of stay for covered hospitalization was 17.8 days). Hospital care and office visits beyond these paid-in-full levels would continue to be covered on a co-insurance basis, but with an increase in the proportion paid by the subscriber from 20 percent to 50 percent.

These proposed changes were a direct reflection of the frustration experienced by local plans in administering our present benefits. As I have indicated earlier, there is a contractual limit on our administrative expenses, so time-consuming and costly reviews of mental claims are difficult to justify. Furthermore, rigorous peer review processes are lacking. We have great difficulty in finding competent mental health professionals who will provide us with meaningful claims review standards or expert testimony when claims are litigated.

The result is that our attempt to provide broad coverage is frustrated, and subscribers are uncertain as to the nature and extent of their coverage. These uncertainties can be removed if we change to a more limited form of coverage, but I do not believe that rigorous definitions and review procedures will be forthcoming soon enough to enable us to keep our present benefit structure.

We have met repeatedly with representatives of the American Psychiatric Association in the hope that this problem could be overcome, but few results have been attained thus far. The lack of progress seems to be attributable much more to the developing nature of the science and practice of psychiatric services than to uncooperative attitudes.

Those analysts who look only at the rather small fraction that mental benefit payments comprise out of total benefits—and thereby conclude that mental benefits are very feasible—are overlooking several key factors. In a period of inflation and economic pressure on employers, employees and third-party payers, no unnecessary costs can be tolerated. Neither can benefit structures be accepted if they lead to wasteful patterns of delivery of services, poor relationships with subscribers or providers, or costly litigation of claims.

Second, the next reason for my pessimism regarding the likelihood of rapid improvement in coverage for mental services stems from the nature of the delivery system—or lack thereof—for mental care.

On this point, the current debate about whether the medical model is most suitable for the provision of mental health services is of fundamental importance. Due to historical precedents and deliberate design, virtually all third-party payers depend upon the physician as the primary legitimator of services. If nonmedical or extramedical models are in fact more appropriate for mental services, then basic changes are called for. New patterns of organization for the delivery of care must be devised and—importantly for third-party financing—become trustworthy in the eyes of the carriers. Alternatively, a new method of financing must be found, which would not rely so heavily upon concepts of diagnosis, treatment and professional supervision.

Interestingly, this differentiation may in part account for the mixed emotions many mental health professionals now exhibit regarding the funding of community mental health centers. *Institutional* support for centers, whether from National Institute of Mental Health grants, local taxes or philanthropy, permits a much wider latitude of operation. Staffing patterns, social services, modalities of service, and so forth, can all be developed with comparative permissiveness. In contrast, if the primary source of funding resides in the eligibility of *individuals* for coverage under an insurance contract, the carrier will make payments based upon claims submitted. For this purpose reliance must be placed upon legitimation of claims by physicians and peer review processes. In passing, it might be noted that health maintenance organizations represent an interesting middle-ground between institutional support and fee-for-service care [2].

In any event, there appears to be a large degree of ferment regarding how mental services can best be delivered. This ferment, while healthy, will probably not permit the development of a symbiotic relationship between insurers and providers in the near future. At the local level, progress will undoubtedly be more rapid, but the extension of local arrangements to national contracts becomes possible only in the presence of recognized accreditation, certification, or other performance-assurance mechanisms.

Third, even if the medical model prevails, there are aspects of mental health care that at present inhibit an improvement of insurance coverage. I'm referring to the difficulty carriers have in obtaining information about the care provided, so that claims payment determinations can be made.

One dimension of this problem arises from the latent or private nature of many services; only the patient and the therapist have direct knowledge of what services were provided, and why. Independent verification of diagnosis or treatment rendered often cannot be obtained from such customary sources as laboratory or X-ray findings, tissue committee reviews, or even autopsies. Thus, the insurer is often left only with the alternative of taking the provider's word—probably an acceptable arrangement *if* meaningful peer review existed.

Another, and to my mind more important, aspect of the "information-gap" problem arises out of the clear need to protect the confidentiality of patient care. Physicians and hospitals have very legitimate concerns about protecting their patients, and especially those receiving mental care. A number of techniques have been devised whereby providers can make available necessary data about the care of patients to insurers. It appears that traditional or conventional procedures, however, may be inadequate for mental services, especially for the payment of service benefits such as those offered by Blue Cross and Blue Shield Plans. The protection of confidentiality—while supplying needed data to insurers—seems to be a problem deserving of high priority collaborative action by both providers and third-party payers.

## SUMMARY

A review of health insurance benefits provided by major third-party payers reveals that mental health services are usually covered. Hospital care is often covered under basic benefits, while cost-sharing through deductibles or co-insurance is usually required for ambulatory services. Limits on hospital days, office visits or dollar amounts payable are frequently employed by carriers as a means of delineating the extent of financial risk to which they will be exposed.

Even in a comparatively generous package of benefits, such as that offered by Blue Cross and Blue Shield Plans to federal employees, mental benefits have proven to be affordable thus far. However, recent concerns over rates and administrative expenses has required carriers to exert the maximum possible control over claims costs. These attempted economies have highlighted the difficulties of providing liberal benefits in the absence of clear definitions and adequate utilization review.

Before major improvements in third-party coverage of mental services can be achieved, dependable mechanisms for quality assurance, preservation of confidentiality, and legitimation of service delivery patterns must be developed. Acting alone, it is impossible for government, the professions and institutional providers, or third-party payers to accomplish what is needed. But if we act cooperatively and aggressively, we can create an accessable, affordable and, above all, effective system for the provision of mental health services.

## NOTES TO CHAPTER SIX

1. See, for example, the following: Follman, J. F., Jr., *Insurance Coverage for Mental Illness* (American Management Association, Inc., 1970); Hall, Charles P., Jr., "The Economics of Mental Health." *Hospital and Community Psychiatry* 21, no. 4 (April 1970): 17–22; Myers, Evelyn S. "Insurance Coverage for Mental Illness: Present Status and Future Concepts," *American Journal of Public Health* 60 (October 1970): 1921–30; Gibson, Robert W., "Can Mental Health Be Included in the Health Maintenance Organization?" *The American Journal of Psychiatry* 128, no. 8 (February 1972): 33–40; Granatir, William L., "Psychotherapy and National Health Insurance," *The American Journal of Psychiatry* 131, no. 3 (March 1974): 267–70; Hall, Charles P., Jr., "Financing Mental Health Services Through Insurance," *The American Journal of Psychiatry* 131, no. 10 (October 1974): 1079–88; Nelson, Scott H., "A New Look At National Health Insurance for Mental Health," *American Journal of Orthopsychiatry* 43, no. 4 (July 1973): 622–28; Spiro, H. R., Crocetti, G. M., and Siassi, I., "Fee-For-Service Insurance versus Cost Financing: Impact on Mental Health Care Systems," *American Journal of Public Health* 65, no. 2 (February 1975): 139–43; and Reed, N., Myers, E., and Scheidemandel, P., *Health Insurance and Psychiatric Care: Utilization and Cost* (Washington, D.C.: American Psychiatric Association 1972).

2. Goldensohn, Sidney S., and Haar, Esther, "Transference and Countertransference in a Third-Party Payment System (HMO)," *The American Journal of Psychiatry* 131, no. 3 (March 1974): 256–60.

Chapter Seven

# A Comparison of Some American and British Models of Community Mental Health Programs

*Norman Rosenzweig*

While many community mental health programs developed in the United States owe a great deal to ideas originating in Britain, the general character of systems of mental health care delivery in the two countries has been quite different and in each case reflects social, cultural, and economic differences between them. A major distinction is the fact that the British system developed in an evolutionary manner as a pragmatic empirical attempt to cope with difficult practical problems of mental health care; while the system in the United States represented a revolutionary introduction of theoretical principles derived in part from various research studies of the relationship between social and environmental causes of mental illness, and partly from a particular political philosophical position. Indeed, the advent of community psychiatry in the United States was hailed as the "Third Psychiatric Revolution."

In Great Britain the community orientation was a direct outgrowth of the efforts to cope with the problems of overcrowding of the mental hospitals. The new National Health Service, born in the period following World War II, was expected to provide free health care to everyone. This included psychiatric care; but the mental hospitals where such care was provided were run-down and already jammed with patients, and the government did not have the money

*Norman Rosenzweig, M.D., is Chairman of the Department of Psychiatry at Mt. Sinai Hospital in Detroit, and Chairman of the APA Council on International Affairs.

Dr. Rosenzweig received his M.D. at Chicago Medical School and did his psychiatric training at Kings Park Hospital in New York. He is a Professor of Psychiatry at Wayne State University and in 1969 he spent a sabbatical in England studying community mental health programs. His recent book is titled, "Community Mental Health Programs in England: An American View."

needed to build new hospitals adequate to the needs. Mental hospital superintendents, faced with the problem of rising admission rates and inadequate hospital facilities, were forced to improvise alternatives to hospital care. The first efforts were directed toward reducing the number of admissions by helping families to care at home for persons who otherwise would have required hospitalization. Later, with the advent of the tranquilizers, most innovations were designed to accelerate the discharge of patients already hospitalized. Emphasis shifted from prevention of hospitalization to rehabilitation and aftercare of discharged mental patients.

In the United States, on the other hand, the community orientation did not develop through the efforts of the hospital superintendents. Indeed, for the most part they opposed it. Rather, community psychiatry was the product of planned change within a particular philosophical framework.

Although mental institutions in the United States were as crowded and inadequate as those elsewhere, American psychiatrists were apparently more complacent. Those in private practice were comfortable with the steady rise in their middle-class clientele for whom psychotherapy had become increasingly fashionable; while those in the institutions were either content to maintain the *status quo*, or else emigrated to private practice.

The initiative for change was taken by the government with the enactment of the Community Mental Health Center Construction Act of 1963. The implementation of the new law was conditioned by the philosophy of community action to solve social problems. As a consequence, community psychiatry became equated with social psychiatry. There was a progressive shift away from the medical model and away from the direct relationship between the psychiatrist and his patient. Increasingly, the skills of the social psychiatrist represented sharp departures from the role definitions psychiatrists developed during their medical education, so that many of them viewed the new approach as alien to their background and orientation. Community psychiatry seemed to be a redirection of mental health efforts towards the solution of social rather than mental illness problems. Most important, while the British system evolved from innovations created by the doctors themselves, the American system was imposed by governmental fiat as a sudden social change.

We have been hearing how the government and other social planners have further revolutionary changes in health care delivery in store for us. There is talk of national health insurance and fear of socialized medicine. Many people are unaware that the British system of health care was not imposed as a social revolutionary event, but actually is the product of a gradual evolution having its roots as far back as the Middle Ages.

In medieval times, the various town councils had responsibility for issuing sanitary regulations to protect the public health; while the sick, especially those who were poor, were cared for in hospitals run by the monasteries. But Henry VIII changed the country's religion and abolished the monasteries, and with them the hospitals, leaving his daughter Elizabeth I a legacy of sick poor with no one to care for them. Consequently, a system of "poor law hospitals" was established during her reign, and these institutions proliferated throughout the country over the next three and a half centuries. They are the ancestors of the municipal hospitals of today.

But very often the condition of these institutions was deplorable, and in the eighteenth and nineteenth centuries, citizens' groups got together and founded voluntary community hospitals. Most of the big London hospitals of today were founded and endowed by local citizens during this time as charitable institutions for the sick and the poor.

In 1912 National Health Insurance was introduced in Britain, which covered most illnesses, though not mental illnesses. The government made a serious effort to upgrade the poor law hospitals to provide the necessary services covered under the insurance scheme, but was not very successful, and there was much public dissatisfaction. Therefore, by 1930 administrative responsibility for operating these poor law institutions was turned over to the local governments, called local authorities in Britain. By 1939 London, Manchester, Birmingham, Middlesex and other councils had upgraded these institutions so that they rivalled the voluntary hospitals in these areas.

So, most communities had two types of hospitals: a voluntary hospital where the medical staff was unpaid or "voluntary"; and a municipal or poor law hospital with a salaried staff. Around 60 percent of the nation's beds were in the latter category.

Thus, when the National Health Service was put into effect in 1948, there was already a widespread pattern of employment of physicians in government operated hospitals. The major change was that the central government took over once again, and that now all doctors and hospitals, including psychiatrists and mental hospitals, were brought under the scheme.

The National Health Service was organized as a tripartite—that is, there were 3 distinct categories of caregivers, each group being separately responsible to the Ministry of Health. The first group was the general practitioners. Patients may choose whichever general practitioners they wish, subject to acceptance by the doctor, who is paid according to the number of patients on his list. The average list contains around 2,500 patients; the maximum allowable is 3,500.

The second category is the public health services, operated by the local authorities and supported by local property taxes, or "rates," though with some subsidy from the central government on a matching basis. Because different local government councils have different ideas about what proportion of the taxpayers money ought to be used to underwrite health services, the quantity and quality of such services vary widely from community to community.

The local authority health services include care of mothers and young children, family planning, home nursing, vaccinations and immunization, and establishment of health centers. It also includes the provision of a number of welfare and social services. The local health authorities are responsible for arrangements for prevention of mental illness, securing care for the mentally ill and for providing aftercare services to discharged mental patients. The latter services were the responsibility of the mental health section of the local health authority. A traditional statutory post in the mental health section has been that of the Mental Welfare Officer (MWO). This post is descended from the "overseer of the poor" under the Elizabethan poor laws. In recent years, the MWO has had responsibility for seeing that the mentally retarded were properly cared for, had responsibility for expediting the mentally ill to mental hospitals and also had certain responsibilities for aftercare. While there were no special training requirements, the MWO often had been trained as a mental nurse, although in more recent years, the tendency was to assign the MWO post to social workers in the mental health section.

The third category of caregivers in the National Health Service is the hospital and consultant services. There are over 2,500 hospitals with more than 434,000 beds, almost half of which are psychiatric, and distributed among over 150 mental hospitals.

The vast majority of medical specialists, called "consultants" in Britain, participate in the health services and hold appointments at particular hospitals. The salary scale in 1970 was between $8,300 and $12,600 per year for a full-time hospital consultant. There are certain additional forms of remuneration that may more than double that income. One method is to give distinction awards for "outstanding professional work" and extra duty payments for additional work outside of the hospital. Most commonly, the consultant works for the health services on a part-time basis and spends about one day a week in private practice. This is called the 9/11th's time arrangement and has been the subject of intense recent controversy.

There are about 2,800 psychiatrists in the hospital services of whom slightly more than 1,000 are consultants or fully qualified specialists. The others have a lesser status, many of them in training positions equivalent to residency. Only fully accredited specialists may see private patients.

The health ministry maintains a strict control on the number of consultant positions and training positions in any given specialty. Most consultant psychiatrists work in the mental hospitals; a number of them hold joint appointments, that is in addition to their mental hospital post, they may hold appointments with a general hospital psychiatry department, with a teaching hospital, with a local authority or with some combination of these. There are few full-time teaching positions for psychiatrists since psychiatry is not emphasized in the medical schools.

There is a considerable cultural difference between the two countries in their use of psychiatric services. In the United States, a dual pattern has developed in which the middle class has tended to see psychiatrists privately for milder disorders, while the lower socioeconomic groups have used psychiatric services primarily for severe illnesses that required institutionalization. Like the blue-collared American, a majority of Britons of all classes have tended to steer clear of psychiatry except when they could not avoid doing so.

In Britain, treatment of mild neuroses by psychotherapy is comparatively rare, partly because there are too few psychiatrists and too many patients with major disorders, and also because most British psychiatrists are poorly trained in dynamic psychiatry and tend to be antagonistic to Freudian ideas. The British psychiatrist is more likely to be concerned with retraining functional capacities and social reintegration into community life than he is with reduction of symptoms *per se.* A patient may be free of overt symptoms and still be considered a therapeutic failure because he is unable to work or live independently; another patient who has persistent psychotic manifestations may nevertheless be counted a success because he is able to live with his family and hold a job. The American psychiatrist would be more likely to make exactly the opposite evaluation.

In Britain, if a patient suffers from a mental illness, his general practitioner will attempt to call in the Mental Welfare Officer who is available twenty-four hours a day, seven days a week. After ascertaining the general nature of the problem, the MWO will arrange either for the patient's evaluation at an outpatient clinic or for a psychiatric consultant to visit the patient at his home. If admission to the hospital is decided upon, the patient will usually be under the care of the consultant who did the evaluating. Only consultants may make such home visits. Those on a part-time arrangement are paid for all home visits they make while those who are on full-time are not paid for the first eight home visits each quarter.

If the psychiatrist decides against admission to the hospital, he may return the patient to the care of his general practitioner with advice for future treatment. He may arrange for the patient to be seen in an outpatient clinic or he may refer the patient to any local authority service that may be available. If the patient is admitted to the hospital, following his discharge he may be referred to a day hospital, industrial rehabilitation unit, or other post-hospital rehabilitation facility operated by the hospital itself, or he can be referred for aftercare services or he may be referred to the care of his former practitioner.

The tripartite division of the National Health Service has made it impossible to develop a consistent national program of community mental health. Although the Ministry of Health has repeatedly emphasized that the mental hospital is but one segment of a comprehensive approach to the treatment of the mentally ill, a division of responsibility has remained between the mental hospital services and those developed within the community itself. There are wide disparities in the amount and type of service provided by the local authorities. Most communities provide only minimal services to the mentally ill. In some instances, the vacuum was filled by the mental hospital; in many cases, it simply remained. Where services are provided, it is not always clear which responsibilities properly belong to the local authority and which to the mental hospital.

There have been, however, unique, original efforts to establish continuity of care which fall into three categories: extension of hospital programs into the community, using hospital staff to operate clinics or day treatment services; development of community programs such as day centers or sheltered workshops by the local authority, using the psychiatric social work staff; and genuine collaboration and joint participation of mental hospital staffs with the resources and manpower of the local authority.

Many of these programs have shown commendable resourcefulness and ingenuity. But they have developed in spite of rather than because of the bureaucratic system, and if a truly comprehensive national program is to emerge, some fundamental changes must take place. Some changes have occurred in recent years, not all with beneficial effects.

In 1971, as a consequence of an extensive study of the local authority social services called the Seebohm Report [1], social workers from the local authority children's department, Welfare Department, and the Mental Health Section of the Health Department were brought together under a single agency called the Local Authority Social Service Department. This department now has responsibility for all mental health functions formerly administered by the Medical Officer of Health. Under this new scheme social workers no longer function in their specialized roles but all are required to function as "generic social workers." Psychiatric social workers, who had constituted a small elite corps of usually better-trained workers, were greatly outnumbered by workers from the other two areas. In addition, all former Mental Welfare Officers, whether or not they had been social workers, were absorbed in the new unified Social Service Department and were expected to per- form as generic social workers. The functions formerly carried out by the MWO are now assigned to members of the Social Service Department, usually without regard for the worker's training or interest in psychiatry or mental health.

Paradoxically, the creation of the new unified department, which was intended to improve the quality and continuity of personal social services, had the effect of damaging severely those community mental health programs operated chiefly by the psychiatric social workers of the local authority. Another consequence has been to strip the Medical Office of Health of many of his responsibilities. Previously a prime agent in motivating the local authority to support mental health programs, he is no longer a viable spokesman for the cause of mental health in the chambers of local government.

On April 1, 1974, two other changes were implemented, which, it was hoped, would have a more stabilizing effect. These [2] are alterations of the pattern of local government in England by changing the geographic boundaries of former counties and boroughs and thereby creating new local authorities; and the reorganization of the Ministry of Health [3], which is intended to eliminate the tripartite structure of the National Health Service and to establish new area health authorities, which now correspond in number and area to the new local authorities. This is an attempt to set up a coordinated regional health care delivery system. Because of the present de- pressed economic conditions, it is difficult to gauge the effects of these changes as yet. However, many doctors have complained that the changes have brought more problems than benefits, and have resulted in increased control of medical care by nonmedical admini- strators.

In addition to the lack of a consistent pattern of community men- tal health services, certain groups have often received less than their due, particularly emotionally disturbed and autistic children and mentally ill senior citizens. The mentally retarded have generally fared better because many local authorities have elected to concentrate their resources in this area in preference to dealing with the mentally ill.

Where services for emotionally disturbed children are available, they fall into one of three categories: child guidance clinics operated by the local authorities and staffed by educational psychologists and social workers; so-called "joint clinics," in which a health service psychiatrist augments the local authority staff, usually on local authority premises; and child psychiatric clinics, based chiefly in general hospitals and operated by the health service. The latter, which have the best trained psychiatrists and the only training posts in child psychiatry, also operate the only inpatient facilities for these children. Austistic children are put into a completely separate category. The local authority provides no ambulatory services for them, and hospital facilities are few and far between.

Psychiatrists have long recognized that mental health services for children are properly a medical responsibility. The recent reorganization of the National Health Service places responsibility for all psychiatric services with the Health Service. A 1973 discussion paper from the Health Ministry [4] recommends that child psychiatric services be developed as part of the district general hospital services.

In view of the shortage of child psychiatrists, a British Psychological Society report has advocated the trebling of educational psychologists to perform the work of the unavailable psychiatrists [5]. It would seem more appropriate, however, to increase medical training efforts to produce the required number of child psychiatrists.

Hopefully, these new developments will improve psychiatric services for emotionally disturbed and autistic children. There are practically no facilities for adolescents, but the Health Ministry has now issued guidelines for development of both inpatient and outpatient services for adolescents.

The accumulation of elderly patients in mental hospitals has threatened to undermine efforts to reduce the number of occupied inpatient beds and has stimulated the development of special geriatric hospitals containing so-called "psycho-geriatric units" for the mentally ill aged patient. Other approaches have included elaborate programs to maintain old people in the community as long as possible with the aid of day centers, day hospitals, "Holiday care," and so forth. The latter is a program whereby the hospital admits the patient for brief periods to give family members some respite, with the understanding that the relatives will resume their responsibility within a specified time, or after a domestic crisis has passed.

It appears to me that some of the new structural changes will bring the British pattern of community mental health service closer to its American counterpart. I believe that although this will necessitate the sacrifice of some excellent existing patterns of care, the overall result will be marked facilitation of continuity of care and integration of effort.

The incumbent psychiatric leadership in the Health Ministry is committed to the strategy of basing major inpatient programs for the mentally ill in district general hospitals [6]. This trend will inevitably constrict the role of large free-standing mental institutions. The mental hospitals will probably not be phased out altogether, as had initially been anticipated in some quarters; the "deteriorated" long-term patient, unable to function without continuous care and supervision, as well as the growing so-called psycho-geriatric population, will most likely be dealt with in these facilities. In the future, however, the majority of new cases and the younger mentally ill population will probably never see the inside of these traditional institutions.

Dr. A. A. Baker, major architect and spokesman for the policy of reliance on general hospital psychiatric departments, has himself had personal experience with the effectiveness and potential of such units [7]. Therefore I expect that, despite some voices of protest or attacks from the press [8], the mental health effort will continue to be concentrated upon the general hospitals.

Emphasis upon the general hospital will of course have multiple consequences for the entire community mental health program at a number of levels. First, basing the psychiatrist in the community rather than at some outlying institution will bring him into more immediate proximity with the programs and problems in the community, and will alter basic patterns of psychiatric practice; psychiatry will become more community oriented and less hospital-oriented. I expect that the majority of mental health problems in the community, particularly acute cases, will increasingly be seen by psychiatrists as medical-psychiatric problems rather than regarded as social service problems. Psychiatrists will give greater emphasis to prevention, with the development of crisis-intervention services and perhaps, some efforts at early case-finding. Therapeutic intervention is likely to become more prompt and more intensive, while length of in-hospital stay will continue to decrease. The British will accustom themselves to the "revolving door" and will recognize, as we have in the United States, that several short in-hospital periods are preferable to a single long one, in terms of economy as well as reduction of the consequences of institutionalism. Day hospital programs will, I believe, become integral components of general hospital psychiatric services, and ambulatory services (already widely available) will receive greater emphasis as an alternative to hospitalization.

Basing mental health care at general hospitals will most likely bring the psychiatrist into closer proximity with his other medical colleagues, although one cannot assume that this will definitely be the case. Psychiatric units, as they exist today in the general hospitals in England, continue to be rather isolated from other hospital facilities and activities, and there is little professional exchange between psychiatrists and other physicians. To some extent this reflects a mutual wish for separation.

The granting of the charter of the Royal College of Psychiatrists in 1971, following a ten year struggle, should do much to enhance the status of psychiatrists within the medical profession. As they lose some of their self-consciousness about their medical identity, they will begin to offer their services to other areas of the hospital. If this occurs, I am certain that there will be a gradual rise, however grudging, in the stature of psychiatry in the eyes of the medical profession. As psychiatry demonstrates its relevance, it will be called upon more frequently. Since emotional complications often accompany somatic illness, patients from elsewhere in the hospital may be transferred temporarily to the psychiatric unit, requiring internists and surgeons to set foot in this alien province. Psychiatrists and their medical colleagues will have a chance to know each other better.

While some psychiatrists will continue to regard their province as the institution rather than the community, and will conduct the general hospital psychiatric unit as if it were merely the old mental hospital moved to a new location, it is difficult to imagine that most psychiatrists based at general hospitals will be unresponsive to community needs. I think they will have neither the resources nor the inclination, however, to become involved in retraining and resocialization programs, let alone the operation of special living accommodations, such as hostels or halfway houses, now operated by social workers.

The arrival in the community of psychiatric personnel to man the new general hospital programs, as well as forthcoming changes in medical education, will eventually have a considerable impact on the general practitioner in Britain.

The American must keep in mind that while psychiatry has become an increasingly important part of the medical school curriculum in the United States over the past two decades, the average British general practitioner has had very limited exposure to psychiatry in his formal training. In addition to his unfamiliarity with psychiatric precepts and practice, he often shares the antipsychiatric prejudices of his nonpsychiatric specialist colleagues, although perhaps to a lesser extent. The average general practitioner is certainly aware that the majority of his patients present emotional symptoms along with their somatic complaints and that some of their somatic symptomatology is entirely emotional in origin, but he is not likely to think of the psychiatrist until his patient is sick enough to require hospitalization.

Another Royal Commission report, the Todd Report [9], promises to have far-reaching effects on medical education. This report seeks to reorganize the present medical school curriculum. Among other things, it seems likely that greater emphasis will be given to subjects related to mental health.

While the Todd Report is expected to have a favorable impact on undergraduate medical education, the need to improve postgraduate training remains. Formalized educational opportunities are not readily available at hospitals outside London. Accreditation of training programs, improvement of libraries, and increased availability of audio-visual teaching aids such as videotape systems are needed. Many British psychiatrists and educators, studying the American model of residency training and board examinations, are pressing for emulation of at least some aspects of the United States system.

The new Royal College of Psychiatrists will determine to a great extent the future content and course of psychiatric education. Present indications are that the examination for admission to the college will be a factual test based on a rigid medical model, which has brought expressions of concern and the recommendation that the examination be kept under critical review [10].

There have been recent political crises that have affected medical care delivery. Under the Wilson Government, the Health Minister has been applying significant pressure to get the consultants to work full time in the health services. The doctors have been resisting these attempts to make them relinquish their private practice; and while not actually striking they are "working to rule," which in effect means that only emergency cases are treated, and the doctor puts in no more than his required eight hours per day regardless of how many patients are waiting to see him. Psychiatrists are united with their colleagues in other specialties in this struggle.

While in the past, doctors who complained about the health services were seeking only to change or improve it, the latest series of difficulties has caused some to express the desire to do away with the system all together.

What does the general public think about this situation? Surprisingly, perhaps, what with the overall economic problems that Britain faces, the public seems largely on the side of the doctors. They see the doctors as another "group of workers" who are being harrassed by the government. Further, although almost everyone uses the health services, which is free to all, most people wish to retain the opportunity to consult a physician privately. There is a story about a man who consulted a physician because he was having difficulty falling asleep. The physician gave him some pills, which worked wonders. The man exuberantly told his friend, another insomniac, how the pills not only put him to sleep but all night long, he dreamed he was on a South Sea Island being pursued by beautiful girls. His friend, too consulted that physician. However, he returned the next day to the doctor to complain, "The pills put me to sleep allright, Doctor, but all night long I dreamed that I was on an island being chased by lions. Why is it that I have this dream whereas my friend, whom you also treated, dreams he is being chased by beautiful women?" Replied the Doctor, "You came to me as a health service patient, but your friend consulted me privately.

Although we have focused our attention on the problems of the British system, the American should keep in mind that community mental health services in the United States have numerous problems of their own, many of them similar to those of the British. Further it would seem that the British have been much more innovative and better prepared to cope with problems than we have been in the United States. In fact, in some respects Britain is answering simple human needs in ways that we in the United States are not. We could well borrow ideas and methods from several of their programs such as the Citizens' Advice Bureaux, which provide help to anyone with a question or problem; hospitals for terminally ill patients; industrial therapy programs; therapeutic social clubs; and direct personal supportive services within the community, such as well-supervised sheltered living accommodations, "meals on wheels," and home helps [11].

The major difference in social organization of the two countries makes any comprehensive replication of their system of social services impossible. Since social services in Britain are organized as a governmental function, an otherwise admirable program may be impossible to emulate in our country. While Britain is a "welfare state," committed to providing social and health services for its citizens from the "cradle to the grave," the United States sees itself as a country of self-made citizens. Americans are expected to be independent and self-reliant, and one is frequently looked down upon if he requires assistance from a social agency or charitable organization, and particularly if he is dependent on government welfare for his support.

As Britain struggles with its economic, political and organizational problems, I have ventured to predict some of the consequences of the recent attempts at planned change.

Unquestionably, there will be further upheavals surrounding the health service reorganization reminiscent of those that followed implementation of the Seebohm report. Particularly, the current economic situation will have far reaching effects. These will, I believe, be transitory, and in the long run, the reorganization will be seen as beneficial.

It would be hazardous to make detailed predictions about local situations, because as we have already noted, much depends on the imagination and energies of those charged with implementing a particular program. If the past is a reliable guide, however, we have reason to expect that British inventiveness and ingenuity will again rise to the occasion and that psychiatry as a whole will be the better for it.

## NOTES TO CHAPTER SEVEN

1. Seebohm, F., chmn, *Report of the Committee on Local Authority and Allied Personal Social Services*, Cmnd. 3703, (London: H.M.S.O., 1968–69).

2. Great Britain, *Royal Commission on Local Government Reform in England*, Cmnd. 4039 (London: H.M.S.O., 1969).

3. Great Britain, Secretary of State for Social Services, *National Health Service Organization: England*, Cmnd. 5055 (London: H.M.S.O., 1972).

4. Great Britain, Ministry of Health, *Discussion Paper on Child Psychiatric Services* (London, 1973), pp. 1–10.

5. Howells, J. G., *Family Psychiatry for Child Psychiatrists* (London: The Society of Clinical Psychiatrists, 1972).

6. Great Britain, Department of Health and Social Security, *Hospital Services for the Mentally Ill*, H.M. (71) 97 (London: H.M.S.O., 1971).

7. Baker, A. A., "Do We Need Psychiatric Hospitals?" in *What's Wrong with the Mental Health Services*? Report of the Annual Conference (London: National Association for Mental Health, 1968), pp. 16–22.

8. "NHS, Diagnosis for a Cure: An Injection of Political Will," *Sunday Times Weekly Review*, May 20, 1973, pp. 33–34.

9. Great Britain *Royal Commission on Medical Education Report 1965–1968*, Cmnd. 3569 (London: H.M.S.O., 1968).

10. Tetlow, C., *Neglected Aspects of Psychiatric Education* (London: Society of Clinical Psychiatrists, 1973).

11. Rosenzweig, N., *Community Mental Health Programs in England: An American View* (Detroit: Wayne State University Press, 1975), pp. 173–84.

## REFERENCES

Dornhurst, A.C. and Hunter, A. 1967. "Fallacies in Medical Education," *Lancet* 2: 666–67.

Ellul, J. 1965. *The Technological Society.* New York: Random House.

Great Britain. Ministry of Health. 1962. *A Hospital Plan for England and Wales.* Cmnd. 1604. London: H.M.S.O.

Hill, Sir Dennis. 1969. "Psychiatric Education during a Period of Social Change," *Brit. Med. J.* 1: 205–09.

Joint Commission on Mental Illness and Health. 1961. *Action for Mental Health.* New York: Basic Books.

Lawless, J. 1971. "The Role of the Medical Profession as an Elite," *Lancet* 1: 543.

Platt, L. 1967. "Medical Science: Master or Servant?" *Brit. Med. J.* 4: 439–44.

Woodmansey, A.C. 1970. "First Principles in Psychiatric Education," *Lancet* 1: 610–11.

Chapter Eight

# Federal Legislation and Mental Health Care

*William Roy **

There are at least two issues of national policy on mental health service planning that are of major importance to psychiatrists and other mental health professionals and workers. One issue is the substantive issue of what is the best mental health system that can be established within the recognized constraints of cost. The other issue is the procedural issue of what can mental health professionals do to assure to the maximum degree possible that the agreed upon system will be assisted by present federal legislation and future national health insurance legislation.

These two questions are the questions that my legislative assistant and I asked again and again about health issues during my service in Congress, and these are the two questions now being asked in many of the offices and committees of Congress today:

"What should be done" in the interest of good mental health care for the American people?

"Is it politically possible?"

First, a couple of disclaimers: Just because a member or committee of Congress is asking what should be done does not mean that the individuals asking the question necessarily assume that the achieve-

*William Roy, M.D., L.L.D., is Director of Medical Education and Professional Services at the St. Francis Hospital in Topeka, Kansas. From 1971 to 1975, Dr. Roy was a member of the U.S. House of Representatives from the 2nd District of Kansas.

Dr. Roy received his M.D. at Northwestern University and his law degree at Washburn University. From 1955 to 1970, he was in the private practice of Obstetrics and Gynecology in Topeka, Kansas. He is a Diplomate of the American Board of Obstetrics and Gynecology and a Member of the Kansas Bar. While in Congress, he was an author of the Health Maintenance Organization Act of 1972 and the major author of the National Health Planning and Development Act of 1974.

95

ment of the goal is in substantial part or in whole a federal responsibility and federal role. It does mean—or at least it so meant in my
former office—that federal actions should be complimentary to private and other governmental actions in reaching such goals rather
than obstructive of such goals. Neither does it mean that either the
goal or method of reaching goals is unchangeable but rather only that
as an attorney might state, these are current conclusions based on the
"best evidence" now available.

Now this may all sound pretty indefinite and intangible. So it is.
Both the determination of what is the most desirable mental health
system and what is the most politically advantageous route for
achieving this system are subject to change—just as mental health and
the theories of the pathogenesis and therapy of mental disease are
subject to change.

Mental health professionals should be best able to determine the
mental health system that is most desirable. Legislators, based on this
professional information and upon the political facts of life as perceived by them, should be most able to determine the most effective
legislation that will achieve these goals.

While I am neither a mental health professional nor at this time a
legislator, it is my purpose here to use the knowledge that I have
gained as a result of medical training, legislative experience, and
personal concern to contribute to this volume on mental health
issues.

In the past, Congress has looked to psychiatrists, psychologists,
administrators, and others to ascertain an effective federal role in
establishing universally available, high quality, mental health services.
They have concluded that there should be a National Institute of
Mental Health to assist in research efforts to find the nature and
treatment of mental diseases.

The Congress has concluded that mental health care needs in this
nation can be effectively met by the establishment of community
health centers distributed on a geographic basis throughout the
nation. Some 2,000 plus were proposed and less than 600 have been
established due to some congressional ambivalence and the pressure
of other priorities requiring federal expenditures. In addition, the
Congress has decided that problems of alcoholism and drug addiction
are closely related to mental disease and that common administration
of such federal programs and the utilization of community mental
health centers for diagnosis and treatment of alcohol and drug problems made good sense. As a result, we have the Alcohol, Drug, and
Mental Health Administration, the ADAMHA.

Payment under Medicare and proposed payment mechanisms for

mental health under national health insurance reveal current thinking within Congress about the nature and treatment of mental disease and the presently favored system for providing mental health service.

Community mental health centers, in spite of a paucity of financial support, are still looked upon with favor within Congress. This is evidenced by the fact that most of the major national health insurance proposals provide for payment for services, often on a preferential basis, provided by a community mental health center. The concept of community-based facilities, with their emphasis on community-based services along a spectrum from preventive care to inpatient care, is still believed valid by influential members of Congress. It is further evident that, while Congress favors this concept, it is not its intention to rely entirely upon it to force all individuals seeking services into the community mental health center pattern.

Major debate and discussion focus on which population groups, and which categories of illness, will be covered under a national health plan and under a community mental health center plan. Some proposals have confined payment to individuals with abject mental illness patterns, while other approaches take a broader perspective and provide payment for less acute emotional and behavioral difficulties. An effort is being made by federal legislators and staff to create a definition, or at least a standard, by which treatment will be made available and paid for. For example, under applicable provisions of H.R. 1 (Chairman Al Ullman's and the American Hospital Association's bill) comprehensive health care benefits shall *not* cover charges for inpatient treatment of mental illness *unless* the "condition is an acute stage and subject to active medical treatment." The term "active treatment" is defined as treatment which "must be (i) characterized by a written and individualized plan that is based on diagnoses; (ii) based on goals relative to arrest, reversal, or amelioration of the disease process or illness and aimed at restoring the individual's adaptive capacity to the maximum extent possible; (iii) based on objectives relating to such goals; (iv) comprised of defined services and activities; (v) specific as to the means to measure the prognosis or outcome; and (vi) clear as to periodic review and revision of the plan." Obviously, benefits under this proposal shall not be made available except to those individuals who are mentally ill and *"acutely"* mentally ill.

Under the provisions of H.R. 21 (introduced by Congressman Corman and concurrently by Senator Kennedy—S. 3—on January 14, 1975) sets a standard of coverage for a psychiatric (mental health) service to an outpatient "only if it [mental health service] constitutes an active, preventive, diagnostic, therapeutic, or rehabilitative service with respect to emotional or mental disorders," and further provides that the patient is covered when services are furnished by a group practice organization (HMO), by a hospital, or by a community mental center, or other mental health clinic, or day care service center. A review of these two standards shows that they are quite different—dramatically different—in the sense that under the first proposal a patient will receive psychiatric services only if he is in an acute status, while under the latter proposal, services are covered when they are given in terms of a more global notion of prevention, diagnosis, therapy or rehabilitation parameters.

It seems to me that the differences in approach in terms of the two proposals cited previously are not only those concerned with political philosophy or understanding of a national health plan approach, but speak directly to the following issue: What is the nature of mental illness, and if we know what it is, how can we successfully treat it?

It seems to me that the answer to this basic, and perhaps over-simplified question, is simply not available and, more to the point, is not available to the mental health professionals who provide the treatment for mentally ill individuals. The central issue is how can the plan for treatment of the mentally ill, under a nationally oriented program, be successful without a determination made as to the nature of mental illness and the vast treatment techniques and procedures for the resolution of such an illness. The mental health professions, nevertheless, are not able, to my knowledge, to answer these questions at this time. Yet, the mental health profession cannot afford to wait for an answer while national health plans continue to be legislated and thereafter implemented.

Therefore, a far-reaching and more global approach, emphasizing, in a national health insurance plan, *not* the specific, but rather a broadly based treatment approach, is the direction that, it seems to me, the mental health community prefers at this time. As an example, the treatment facilities, historically, for the mentally ill have been concentrated in two primary areas: first, the state mental hospital, and second, the privately practicing psychiatrist. In the latter (private practice), the emphasis has been on psychotherapy, which includes supportive, directive, or expressive psychotherapy procedures aimed at resolving emotional difficulties encountered by persons who are functioning marginally or relatively well in their day-to-day activities. Psychoanalysis, a more long-term and more ambitious psychotherapeutic technique, is included in this category.

On the other hand, the state hospital systems have been the treatment facility for the typically nonfunctioning, acutely ill, psychiatric patient, whose destiny is determined largely in terms of custodial care, with only marginal progress being the prognosis under a treatment plan, which may or may not include some form of therapeutic intervention.

In the late 1950s and in the early 1960s, the picture changed drastically and culminated in the passage of the Community Health Centers Act of 1963, which implemented a notion that the resources of the community could be mobilized to provide a *different type of treatment modality* for the mentally ill. The approach under the community mental health centers program has more to do with the *broad range of treatment intervention techniques,* rather than new information or advances in psychiatric knowledge or treatment methods. As an example, over the last decade, while the community approach has been implemented, community mental health centers are mandated, and do in fact provide, a whole range of services—including inpatient, rehabilitation, preventive, family service, consultation, and drug therapy programs—all aimed at the provision of mental health services that will encompass a treatment plan for the entire range of emotional or psychiatric difficulties the individual and his family encounter. Perhaps the major shift that has resulted from the community mental health centers approach has been the ability of the mentally ill individual and his family *to avoid inpatient custodial care* in a state hospital, except in cases of nonfunctioning behavior for which the inpatient facilities of the mental health center are not available.

Many knowledgeable persons in the field continue to debate the basic merits of the community-based approach and believe that the community-based approach is not the best answer available for the treatment of mental illness. At the present, however, the status of mental health services in the United States seems to involve a balance of three treatment modalities: the state hospital system, community mental health centers, and private practice of psychiatry. The passage of national health insurance will change the balance of these three treatment approaches. *Resources* for the treatment of the mentally ill will *follow according to the financial resources available* for treatment. Should the Congress emphasize inpatient care, or alternately, the community approach, or increase the number of covered visits to the privately practicing mental health professional, the payment mechanism will provide the basis for the day-to-day decisions of where and by whom patients will receive mental health care.

Basic questions persist—despite the introduction of national health plans—in terms of the *effectiveness* of certain types of mental health treatment procedures. For example, the following questions pertain:

Is the long-term psychotherapeutic approach the preferred method of treatment; is the long-term institutional setting the only treatment facility for the chronically ill (or is drug maintenance and drug therapy just as good); is crisis intervention really the best that can be expected in terms of a community's mental health needs; should the mental health profession be concentrating not so much on the individual but on his family and extended family situation; is, with yet another step, the work and geographical environment of the individual and his family the primary area of emphasis in which productive change will occur with the proper treatment approaches; should the mental health professionals be concentrating on even larger systems and work with so-called "normal" individuals and groups, in terms of their business and industrial environments; should at the other end of the spectrum, the mental health profession be concentrating primarily on prevention at an early age rather than dealing with crisis when it develops; and should the major focus center on the children and adolescents whose personality and character patterns will determine their mental health status when reaching adulthood? Another critical question that remains unresolved is what is the connection between physical and mental illness: Should physical and mental illness be treated the same under a national health plan; is there a critical and measurable relationship between a person's physical illness and his mental health status; do other physicians become confronted in many, many cases with problems of mental illness that are diagnosed as physical illness; would a concentrated effort on prevention of mental illness result in a reduction of physical symptoms and reduce need for resolution of so-called "physical" ailments?

This series of questions addresses the etiology and treatment of psychiatric disease, including prevention of disease and relationship to ailments usually categorized as physical ailments.

Another series of questions that must be answered before writing the benefit package of national health insurance is who will be paid for providing mental health service?

What role should the auxiliary mental health professions play in the provision of mental health services—that is, should a national health plan give equal coverage to a clinical psychologist, social workers, psychiatric nurses and psychiatric aides on parity with psychiatrists in the delivery of mental health services to mentally ill individuals? A legislative provision in point is H.R. 3674 (The National Health Security Act) introduced by Representative Matsunaga on February 25, 1975. Under the provisions of H.R. 3674, the emphasis in the bill has been shifted from "psychiatric" care to "mental health" care and the definition of physician is expanded to include psychologist. The bill covers "the professional services of a practitioner who is a certified or licensed psychologist, furnished in any state, if such services are of a kind which that state authorizes to be furnished by such practitioners." Should similar provision be made for the psychiatric social worker, and psychiatric registered nurse, and psychiatric aide? Will a national health insurance plan subsidize the privately practicing M.D.–psychiatrist, and omit the professional abilities of the psychologist, social worker, and other mental health professionals? Can a national plan adequately serve the mental health needs of the American population if coverage services include only those of a medical doctor and not those of otherwise qualified mental health professionals especially if the general tenor of the national plan is community based and is one that emphasizes treatment under a global plan to assist, not only individuals, but families, children, schools, courts, and other community institutions?

A third series of questions and decisions pertains directly or indirectly to the site of treatment. What should the proper role be for the general hospital; and if the general hospital contains an active psychiatric unit, should such a unit be an isolated and separate part of the on-going activities of that general hospital or should its facilities be integrated into the treatment area designed for care of those with physical difficulties; will greater community understanding and lessened community fear of mental illness make the community outpatient setting an increasingly appropriate site for mental health care; if health insurance benefits do not pay for long-term care will states continue to maintain mental hospitals for providing care for the chronically mental ill; is a plan for psychiatric and mental health care to all citizens *feasible* in terms of the enormous magnitude of the problem; who should pay for psychiatric care—that is, is it a responsibility for the general taxpayer who will pay for mental health services in terms of taxes under a social security trust fund arrangement, or is it rather more properly suited for payment under some kind of third party arrangement and a private insurance plan, or is some combination of both to be preferred; should a psychiatrist, and other mental health professionals, confine themselves to clinical matters only, or should they, on the other hand, involve themselves in administrative, political, and community reforms that are relevant to *delivery* of mental health services to those communities in which they live; what is the status and the outlook for psychiatric (M.D.) residency training programs, and training programs for the psychiatric social worker and registered nurse, as well as the psychologist who is desiring to practice in the mental health field? Further, what will be the impact of judicial decisions concerning patients' rights, the right-to-treatment, the right to no treatment, and malpractice suits concerning the adequacy of psychiatric care?

Finally, there are the questions intrinsic to the entirety of the debate on national health insurance, with the special question about whether benefits for psychiatric and mental health care are either initially or in the long term feasible. Perhaps the magnitude of the problems of mental health is too great to include comprehensive or nearly comprehensive benefits in a national health insurance plan.

The single most important question regarding national health insurance is how will the money flow? We know where the money will come from; it will come from all productive and other self-sustaining Americans either in the form of taxes or private health insurance premiums. But we do not know whether or not the money will flow to Washington whereby the federal government will plan centrally for the amount and use of the health care dollar or whether a less formal mechanism will exist whereby all citizens will purchase a mandated benefit package from private sources, and such supplementary private insurance as they believe desirable.

It is in this area that I am highly opinionated. It is my conviction that we as citizens and health professionals must not look to the federal government to pay for all or nearly all health care services. If we do, the federal government will not allocate enough dollars to health care to provide the extent and quality of services that the American people desire and deserve. The federal government has other higher and longer established priorities.

Health care cannot compete in the federal budgeting process with income maintenance, national defense, energy needs, environmental responsibilities, transportation, and a host of other accepted federal responsibilities for the limited number of federal dollars.

There is copious evidence for this. Nearly all federal health commitments of the past have been underfunded. The honeymoon years of the National Institutes of Health are the exception. But currently, NIH money is being reduced, health planning is being dollar starved, PSRO's cannot get the minimal funding necessary, and we all know what is happening to mental health funding.

There is an alternative to federal national health insurance. It is mandated third-party payment for the employed, self-employed, and others with adequate funds or income, which reserves federal dollars for the purchase of the same insurance and the same access to health care for the poor, disabled, and elderly as our other citizens have.

If there is not enough federal health money to go around, it is nearly certain that payment for many mental health services will not be provided for initially and that in any subsequent budget cuts, mental health benefits will be among the first to be cut. Needs and benefits of treatment are too difficult to determine, and, in addition, utilization of benefits is likely to vary greatly throughout the nation.

We need only look to past federal and state actions to confirm this. Certainly, we are all acutely aware of how difficult it is to get state money for state mental hospitals and other programs and, also, which programs are cut first in a state government budget squeeze. So, I repeat, it is unwise to look to federal payment for all or nearly all health care service.

Nor should partial federal programs that establish new mechanisms of federal payment be favored by those of us concerned with obtaining adequate resources for quality health care. We should not look to the federal government to pay for the costs of catastrophic care because such a program establishes a mechanism of payment for all citizens that will extend into perpetuity. The benefits will predictably become greater, either by the ravages of inflation—for example, more bills exceeding, say, $2,000 and therefore a greater proportion of federal payment—or by legislative action such as lowering a $2,000 ceiling for private payment to $1,800 or an "over 8 percent of income" catastrophic provision to an "over 7 percent of income" catastrophic provision.

Nor should we support the federalization of Medicaid separate from comprehensive national health insurance. It has been illustrated again and again the separate programs for the poor are poor programs. The medically indigent of this country should have the same "ticket" for health care as all other Americans even though public monies rather than private monies will purchase the ticket for admission into the system and the purchase of services. Anything less, whether a federal or state-federal program, establishes a two-level system of health care with the lesser level for the poor, disabled, and elderly.

I have been audacious enough to tell what I believe must not be done: support free standing catastrophic health insurance or support a separate albeit federal, program for the poor. I will be bold enough to state some of the things I believe mental health professionals should be doing.

First, they should be answering as well as possible all of the questions posed earlier in this chapter—plus many questions I either have not thought of or have chosen not to include. We all recognize that most of these questions cannot be answered definitely at the present time. But, as I stated earlier, in any society both legislative and legal decisions must often be made following the "best evidence" rule.

Mental health professionals, to the extent possible, should provide legislators with a consensus answer on each question—or at least a majority opinion with minority reports.

Then they must communicate these answers to the members of Congress by a variety of techniques and routes, and at certain critical times.

Let's take the question of timing first. The input of information when possible should precede the drafting and introduction of the legislation. The provisions for mental health coverage in the Ullman and Kennedy-Corman bills were not materialized from nothing. The American Hospital Association and its large and expert staff wrote most of Chrairman Ullman's bill. They relied on experience, litera-ture, written and spoken advice, as well as biases and prejudices in determining the proposed mental health benefits. Some mental health professionals worked with them. I don't know who.

A similar process was used to determine the provisions of the Kennedy-Corman bill. The Committee of One Hundred provided the recommendations that were incorporated into that bill.

In each case, staff of the member of Congress or of the committee that he chairs, Chairman Ullman's Ways and Means Committee, Chairman Kennedy's Health Subcommittee of the Senate Labor and Education Committee, worked with the other interested parties, in this case primarily the AHA and the Committee of One Hundred.

The time of initial drafting prior to introduction is the one best time to influence legislation. Thereafter, legislation may be changed in subcommittee, committee, on the floor of the respective bodies, or in conference where the two bodies iron out differences in their respective bills.

And always the administration in power will have great influence, and thereby be subject to reason and influence, in the writing of legislation. This takes three forms. First, the administration legisla-tive proposal, if there is one (there is no administration national health insurance proposal at this time); two, administration testi-mony and the provision of statistics, evidence, and expertise to the Congress from within the administration; and, three, the threat or use of the presidential veto power.

At each level, subcommittee, full committee, and floor, it becomes more difficult to change legislation, although it is never too late and, occasionally, momentous changes occur because at each succeeding level political awareness, in and out of Congress, and political pres-sures increase. These pressures culminate in conference, and it is at this final level that one person can decide the congressional fate of a legislative issue. But this is the final roll of the dice, and one may be shooting his entire stake.

How do you make input? It is easier in the examples used if you are from the Second District of Oregon or the state of Massachusetts because each legislator, all other things being equal, will look to his constituent for advice. Moreover, his constituent with time, good advice, and perhaps political support, is likely to become his friend, or at least his ally. As you may recall, one recent president said in politics there are no friends, only allies. The Humphrey-McGovern primary spectacle in California in 1972 was an illustration of this.

So, rule one is know and work with the member on a personal basis. Second best is on a professional committee on delegation basis. All members of Congress recognize and evaluate the self-interest of their petitioners, and no group should be shy or apologetic about this. Everyone has certain personal or professional self-interests.

Rule two is if you cannot have a personal relationship with the member, then establish one with his key staff person in your area of interest. I introduced H.R. 14409 in the last Congress and that bill in turn became in great part P.L. 93—641, the Health Planning and Resources Development Act of 1974. My legislative assistant spent most of the hours talking with and reading letters from the identified experts in this area. There are no more than a dozen such highly influential staff people in health on the Hill. They are the information gatherers, technicians, and sometimes even the idealogues of health care legislation.

Testimony before committees is important but less so than one-to-one input. Informing your individual representative and seeking his vote is also very important. But these and other effective actions are of a lesser magnitude than being there when the bill and its amendments are originally drafted.

One final word: Members of Congress are for the most part talented, informed men and women of good will. They welcome you and your help.

In sum, I have been presumptive enough to present two charges to those concerned with planning and funding mental health care: First, find the best answers to a multitude of questions that must be answered as well as possible in order to write workable national health insurance legislation. And, second, communicate these answers to the men and women who will decide the provisions of a national health insurance law. I have presented here some of these questions that can be answered best by psychiatrists and other mental health professionals. And I have hopefully provided some insight as to how this information can be transmitted to the Congress in order to assure the passage of good legislation.

Chapter Nine

# Feasibility and Implications of Insurance for Mental Health

*Henry A. Foley* *

The purpose of my discussion is to sketch out a reasonable position on the feasibility of mental health coverage in a national health insurance program and the implications of that coverage. At the National Institute of Mental Health I was assigned almost exclusively for four years to the study of the feasibility of mental health coverage in insurance plans. I have come to the conclusion that it is unrealistic and unwise to expect that policy formulation in the mental health area can proceed on a "first-best" or "best-of-all-possible-worlds" basis—specifically, unlimited mental health coverage for all populations without third-party intervention or interference. The data that would be needed to formulate truly optimal policies are not available and should not be expected to be available in the foreseeable future. The participants in the mental health system as in any human service delivery system do not or will not behave in the manner that those of us who either advise or indeed formulate policy would like them to behave.

We who formulate policy should rely on the expected responses, or better yet ranges of expected responses, rather than preferred responses when we initiate policy actions either at the federal or State level. We can, of course, and should provide incentives that will

Henry A. Foley is Executive Director, Colorado State Department of Social Services, and former Deputy Director and Planning Chief of the Office of Program Development and Analysis and Senior Economist at the National Institute of Mental Health in Washington, D.C.

Dr. Foley received his doctoral degree at Harvard University where his thesis was entitled, "Politics of the Passage of the Community Mental Health Centers Act." He has been a Consultant on Health Economics to HEW and a health economist at NIMH. He is the author of numerous publications, including "Mental Health and the Poor," Multiple Source Funding," and "Financing Mental Health Care in the United States."

107

leave participants to respond in the generally most favored manner. My statement suggests that today as a policy analyst I will work toward what are sometimes called second-best solutions. In attempting a second-best solution, the analyst explicitly recognizes limitations in achieving everything he wishes to accomplish and formulates a policy that looks best given the limitations of the real world. This second-best bromide is neither a give-up nor a reformist-as-opposed-to-revolutionary doctrine. Indeed, it may lead to more radical policy innovation than would a first-best formulation. In the past I have advocated a type of coverage that may be characterized as rather unlimited in nature. I would now like to make a different statement. A statement somewhat in opposition to the conventional wisdom about the type of coverage we should push for in national health insurance.

My statement is rather simple and is as follows: mental health coverage in a national health insurance program is feasible for definable mental health illnesses that have definable treatments that lead to definable probable outcomes. My statement, as I will explain, is related to the present moment and not to some future point in time when circumstances such as the nature of treatment, the nature of mental illness, and the nature of the economy might very well be changed. Let me explain to you how I have arrived at this statement. An examination of four items will indicate why the position I am suggesting is a realistic position. First, there is the historical development of insurance; secondly, the dynamics around coverage as we know it today in both public and private insurance programs; third, the real constraints on politicing for the provision of mental health coverage in national health insurance; and fourth, the question of the credibility of the mental health professions in their attempt to be included in national health insurance.

During the past 20 years we have seen health insurance companies expand their coverage for care of the mentally ill. Private insurers faced with competition among themselves, various union negotiating groups demanding psychiatric benefits for their membership, the federal government in two of its largest programs—the Federal Employees Health Benefit Plan and the Civilian Health and Medical Program of the Uniformed Services (CHAMPUS)—have pushed and obtained this coverage. Within this period we have seen the careful negotiation of the American Psychiatic Association with officials in the federal bureaucracy to include at least some type of coverage in both the Medicare and Medicaid programs. The change from almost no coverage in 1950 and dependency upon the state hospital system to a situation today in which 100 percent of the Blue Cross plans in this country include at least some coverage for in-hospital treatment of mental illness is indeed remarkable. Most of us know that the major medical policies pioneered by commercial insurers do not have provisions in them that distinguish between various kinds of treatment. Within the major medical policies there is indeed the opportunity for coverage for many of the patients with whom psychiatrists come in contact. Although many people basically unfamiliar with insurance practice are still convinced that the failure to specifically mention the existence of psychiatric benefits means that no coverage exists. This is seldom true under group policies when health benefits are more commonly offered on a comprehensive or all except basis. In other words, unless there is a specific exclusion contained in the policy for psychiatric treatment, on either an inpatient or outpatient basis, coverage does exist.

Where coverage for mental illness is often highly restricted or non-existent is in individually sold policies, and it is in this are that the insurance industry needs to find ways of making adequate coverage available.

Last year a careful examination of both the Aetna and Blue Cross policies under the federal employees' plan revealed that roughly 7 percent of all benefits paid under Federal Employees Health Benefit Plan go directly to treatment of mental illness. This figure is still an insurable level. After twenty years, the question "is mental health insurance feasible" has been replaced by the question "at what levels and for whom should coverage be included?" There are currently at least thirteen proposals for various forms of coverage in the Congress, and more are likely in the next few years.

A problem has arisen, however, concerning what might be called the carte blanche nature of the coverage in both the Federal Employees Health Benefit Plan and the CHAMPUS program. As you may know, in 1974 The Senate Committee on Government Operations, Permanent Sub-committee on Investigations explored the rising amounts and proportions of benefits being paid under the CHAMPUS program for mental health care: 12 percent of total CHAMPUS costs in 1969, 15 percent in 1970, 16 percent in 1971, 18 percent in 1972, and 19 percent in 1973. This experience offers us reason for some caution because the liberal, nondiscriminatory benefits for psychiatric care were clearly abused in this particular insurance program. Information developed during the hearings and other examinations of the program done both at the Defense Department and at the National Institute of Mental Health indicated a gross lack of oversight and review of utilization of mental health services—particularly in long-term residential care settings for children and adolescents. Both the CHAMPUS officials and the insurance carriers responsible for claims administration clearly needed mechanisms for clearer determinations of appropriate treatment, cost containment and quality assurance.

A second program came in for critical review, and this was the Federal Employees Health Benefit program. Both Aetna and Blue Cross–Blue Shield suggested that the increasing costs that were being observed for mental health coverage in their plans were due to lack of restraint or controls on long-term intensive psychiatric therapy. In response to both the CHAMPUS and Federal Employees Health Benefit insurance problems, joint efforts have developed among the federal government agencies—specifically, the National Institute of Mental Health, Civil Service Commission, and Defense Department—and professional associations, providers and the insurers participating in these programs. The problems surfaced both in the Federal Employees Health Benefit Plan and in CHAMPUS caution us to develop boundaries on the type of coverage we may allow in the insurance package for national health insurance. Otherwise, our credibility—specifically our credibility about the type of coverage for mental health care—is at serious risk.

On a more local level, in the past five months of my brief tenure as the Executive Director of the Department of Social Services in the State of Colorado, I have had as one of my responsibilities the Medical Assistance or Medicaid Program. This program reimburses for many of the psychiatric services provided by community mental health centers. There is a tremendous range in the cost of a unit of service for the same type of patient served by the same type of provider across community mental health centers. This too has cautioned me, and my staff is now in the process of negotiating with the community mental health centers and the American Psychiatric Association's chapter in the State of Colorado to arrive at uniform rates for specific units of service for specific types of clients by specific types of providers, providers being physicians as well as psychologists and social workers.

The experience of the CHAMPUS and Federal Employees Health Benefit programs and local medical assistance programs such as Colorado's has brought home to us sooner rather than later that as a profession we must face up to the fact that the insurance mechanism does need some definitions, some parameters, by which it can measure and predict failures and successes. Definitions have been particularly hard to come by in the mental health field. In the past few years the mental health professions have recognized the direct relation between the development of standards and effective review mechanisms and the treatment of mental health care under third-party payment programs, including national health insurance. There are the efforts made by the American Psychiatric Association in its development of model criteria sets for peer review and the specialized standards for accreditation of various types of psychiatric facilities that have been established by the Joint Commission on the Accreditation of Hospitals. All of these efforts are commendatory, and, yet, we realize that the insurers have expressed justifiable concerns about the effectiveness of professional guidance and criteria for determining the necessity, duration, modality, and outcome of treatment.

This leads me to the biggest challenge we face today. Funding authorities as well as insurers are requesting but not receiving answers to hard questions such as: "How much is the population serviced actually benefiting from the services we are paying for?" It seems evident to the askers, and as well as to us, that the effectiveness of the delivery of care must ultimately be assessed in terms of the resulting condition of state of the recipients of the services that are delivered by you and paid for by the funding authorities. How we answer that question will effect the limits on the provision of mental health coverage in a national health insurance program. So far the debate has centered on the number of inpatient and outpatient and partial hospitalization days that should be covered in the national health insurance program and more recently on a careful process of peer review and other quality control mechanisms that take into account and balance both humanitarian and cost control issues. Implementing such a provision on a national scale has tremendous and rather "mind boggling" implications.

A look at the huge obstacles involved in setting up the far more modest Professional Standard Review Organization operation may indicate that peer review, while critical, will not be accepted as the ultimate and immediate solution to the control issue. A major complicating factor is the amount of jockeying by the various mental health professions to be included as providers under national health insurance—psychiatrists, psychologists, social workers, ministers, and "free lancers." Such debate does not seem to educate elected officials on what the mental health professionals are really able to accomplish if they are reimbursed for services under a national health insurance program. That is, indeed, where the discussion or the level of debate must be engaged.

What opened or freed private insurers to cover mental health care in the past 20 years was the development of new technologies such as chemotherapy and new modalities of treatment and new organizational ways of providing that treatment such as community mental health centers. The insurers' understanding of the fact that a person can be maintained through a drug regimen in a functioning state has led them to be more willing to insure for mental health coverage. I suggest to you that specific mental health services for specific populations can be sold under a national health insurance program. Where existing technologies can assist a person with definable illness to arrive at a level of functioning that is reasonable and acceptable to the average person, is where we will be able to convince elected officials that coverage for mental health care makes sense. The American Psychiatric Association *Diagnostic and Statistical Manual of Mental Disorders* (DSM–II) and/or the functional diagnostic scale of Doctors Fishman and Ciarlo can be made to come alive and relevant to the discussion, for it is in this manual or scale that mental health illnesses are defined.

A second step must take place, and that is to tie treatment to diagnosis in the minds of our elected officials. For example, in the area of acute schizophrenia and other acute psychosis we know that medication is appropriate and can be helpful to the functioning of the individual. In the area of alcoholic treatment we are aware we have detoxification programs and anti-abuse programs. In the area of specific phobias, specific behavioral therapeutic techniques have been tried, tested, and discussed. There are behavioral therapy and family therapy techniques for some sexual problems. Brief individual psychotherapy sessions are appropriate for grief reactions prior to depression. We are aware that crisis interventions of one to five visits are appropriate for other acute situational reactions, and it is these types of treatments, which have definite time and probable effectiveness boundaries, that legislators as well as other laymen can comprehend.

The assumption that most legislators read such literature as *Psycho-Today* or the *Psychiatric Annals* or popularization in the press about effective modalities of care may have little basis in fact and less relevance when legislators discuss what should or should not be included under national health insurance as regards mental health coverage. And the second assumption that they will accede in all instances to the guidance of professionals is out dated. Politicians or elected officials face political, economic, and informational constraints in their bargaining for mental health coverage. Their political and economic constraints are as follows:

As they deliberate about the allocation of national or state resources, they are faced with competing groups who demand that the resources they control be allocated to health, as well as mental health, to social services, to a multiple range of human services, as well as other items, such as, highways, national defense, agriculture, and so forth. Among the various items that they must bargain about, mental health insurance currently occupies an inappropriately low position in their debates. This is true despite the fact that most proposals for national health insurance include some provision for mental health coverage. Legislators are affected by the current recession or depression as much as the man on the street. In their deliverations such terms as cost benefits, bottom lines, and global budgeting have become much more prevalent. Economic pressures towards global budgeting for specific medical and social services programs are upon us. Increasingly, legislators are demanding much more careful estimates about the cost of service programs upon which they will vote.

Those elected officials who reside in the Washington community have been influenced by the press concerning the amounts of long-term intensive psychotherapy that has been provided to many of the employees in the federal government in the past three and four years at extremely high cost to the Federal Employees Health Benefits Plan. These politicians encounter many of these persons in care who are functioning quite well not only in the federal bureaucracy, but oftentimes in their own offices, and they raise the legitimate question as to whether psychotherapy for self-actualization purposes is an appropriate therapy to be included under a national health insurance program. That question is not without a context, for many of the legislators are aware that even today most psychiatric patients are seen in the public sector or in a combination of the public and private sector as exemplified in community mental health centers and clinics. They are also aware of such studies as Harvey Brenner's *Economics of Mental Illness* and other such studies which have been written in the past ten years. These studies clearly identify that many of our major mental health problems are identified or associated with persons of the lower-income populations who are unable to afford the care provided by many psychiatrists and psychologists in the private sector.

Too often that population is seen only in public mental hospitals and oftentimes not at all. Consequently, these politicians or elected officials struggle with the issue of how to make an insurance program equitable so that this particular population will certainly receive coverage under a national health insurance program.

The time has come in which we need to clearly delineate a reasonable mental health care cost level for coverage of the total population in the United States wherever they may be located: on the street, in a private office, or even in state mental hospitals. Until recently the available cost data has been of a wide-ranging nature and not often clear. Now the situation is quite different. We now have sufficient experience with a total range of population of all income classes to suggest a valid estimate of what mental health insurance coverage would cost under a national health insurance program if it were enated today.

Based on the experience of the Health Insurance Plan of greater New York ($30.00 per year for a family of 3 or more), the Blue Cross–Blue Shield experience in the United Auto Workers Contracts with Ford, General Motors, and Chrysler ($33.00 to $51.00 per year for a family), and the $14.50 per person, per year experience under Federal Employees Health Benefits, we are able to arrive at what it would cost the country to provide mental health coverage for the total population at risk—that is to say, the total population of the United States. If we assume that the average cost per person per year is $14 and multiply that cost times a population of 225 million Americans, we arrive at a insurance premium cost of 3 billion, 150 million dollars to cover the total population.

If you have read the Levine and Levine study of 1974 you will recall that their estimates, after they had looked at all of the cost data they were able to assemble from various sources in the United States, was $10.4 billion for direct care. You may wonder why the discrepancy between my $3 billion, 150 million figure and their $10.4 billion dollar figure. The explanation is rather simple. The Levine figure includes the fixed cost of state and county hospital systems, other public mental hospital nursing homes, and construction—approximately $6 billion, 379 million. Much of the cost experience in these programs are domiciliary in nature and are not medical. The policy question that such data raise or point to is how we will decide to fund the domiciliary and other social services that are appropriate to these patients within these facilities. What will be the fiscal resources for these essential services? At the same time we should not exclude this large institutional population from coverage for psychiatric services under a national health insurance program.

It is about time that we decide that we must continue to address and solve the issue of integration of the roles and responsibilities— financial and programmatic—of each component of the human service system. It is extremely critical to design and integrate programs of national health insurance, income maintenance, and social services that will serve our physically and mentally disabled. The present nonsystem is composed of disjointed services occasioning lack of care, and lack of support to much of our population. Such problem solving around the integration of services will require more and more the committed collaboration of the physicians in this country. We are past the time of fragmenting our services or of deciding to deal in isolation or of perpetuating insular patterns in the delivery of human services. This challenge is by far the greatest challenge we all face.

I suggest, however, that a clear presentation of mental health coverage at a bottom line cost of $3 billion, 150 million for all Americans is an insurance package acceptable to politicians as long as we alert them and are supportive to their efforts to expand social service support and integrate that support in the delivery of psychiatric medical care to the patient. At the same time that we are presenting a feasible mental health package to be included under national health insurance, it is incumbent upon us to describe mental illness, to define mental illness, to define our treatments, and to define our probable outcomes. By the term probable outcomes, I mean that the professions should be able to indicate the probabilities of persons returning acceptable functioning in our society.

The implications of such an approach are several. First, while we accept the fact that long-term intensive psychotherapy is a legitimate modality for some, it has not proven to be clearly definable in its treatment and in its outcome. More importantly, it is doubtful that elected officials will wish to insure long-term intensive psychotherapy for self-actualization purposes. The profession must self-police itself or the third party, be it the government, or private insurers will cut back on the utilization or on the allowance of the utilization of long-term intensive psychotherapy. In the particular instance of the patient who comes to the mental health professional, it may be unclear if the issue is a situation of crisis intervention or an issue of self-actualization. There are ways to provide safeguards for this type of situation. In the area of outpatient visits, the first five visits under a national health insurance program would be covered at 100 percent by the insurance program, the sixth to the tenth visits perhaps at 80 percent, and the eleventh to the twentieth visits at 50 percent, and then it would become questionable whether from the twenty-first to the $X$ number of visits any coverage should incur under a national health insurance program. This position may seem harsh, but I think that it is reasonable and politically viable. Such a fiscal mechanism assures that the person in a crisis situation will not be deprived of necessary care and discourages a person to embark on the task of extended psychotherapy. Concomitantly the check on the use of long-term intensive psychotherapy for self-actualization purposes obviates the danger that the 3 billion, 150 million dollars would be diverted from the total poulation at risk to a relatively small elite population. The clear danger of covering long-term psychotherapy for self-actualization purposes is that it would absorb an inordinate share of the total portion of national health insurance allocated for mental health care. Such a fiscal probability would endanger the availability of necessary care for the severely ill.

The positive aspect of coverage available to the total population, understandable to elected officials, is that for the first time we will not have populations discriminated against by reason of lack of income or of location in certain facilities or of minority status.

The negative aspect of a victory in achieving coverage for the total population in a national health insurance program is that we would forget that there must be social services support systems that compliment a national health insurance strategy. Supportive services are needed as follows: day care, "meals on wheels," transportation, special education, vocational counseling and training, homemaker services, chore and shopping assistance, protective services, supervised living arrangements, recreation and leisure time activities, and maintenance.

Very close to my office in Denver there are former patients I encounter. They have been either in the state mental hospital system, or in even some of our private hospitals. They have been released to the community. In this concentrated section of Denver, there are two thousand formerly ill patients who at this time receive neither adequate health insurance coverage and certainly almost nonexistent social services. In fact, there is one social worker attempting to provide the multiple range of services I have suggested to those two thousand people. As you know, this is a situation repeated numerous times in California and other states throughout our country. Society's forgotten and ignored ill should incite us to carve out of a national health insurance program what is feasible in the way of medical coverage and push for an expansion of social service support systems, under such programs as Title XX of the Social Security Act and the other Titles of the Social Security Act. We are moving past the time when we can continue to fragment the delivery of services to our population. It is time that we move into a system comparable to the Europeans and the Japanese in which both health care and social service support for all populations—poor, middle class, and rich—are equally available. It is time that we clear the mist on exorbitant costs or the danger of exorbitant cost for mental health coverage. It is time we point out that we are suggesting coverage for definable illnesses, with definable treatments, and with definable outcomes and that we are not asking for coverage for self-actualization purposes for the total American population. We have the behavioral ability to define outcomes, now increasingly demanded by third-party sources. Increasingly we will use those definitions.

I would caution us not to take an incremental strategy that would suggest that what we initially do in a national health insurance plan is phase in children, and then juveniles between 13 and 21, and then populations above 21, and then populations above 65. Why? It is clear that if one is going to treat a person with a familial problem of a psychiatric nature that more and more of the total family unit must be treated and to try to gerrymander the system so that the provider must bill against the child or bill against the parent or bill against one spouse rather than another is dysfunctional, dishonest, and probably a disservice to both the providers and the patients. It is time we explained the range of individual and family therapies that we have available to us so that our legislators will insure a package that they themselves or members of their families or friends may someday have need of.

The basic issues arising out of the national health insurance debate will, in my opinion, be resolved successfully only to the extent that there is clear understanding of what definable mental illnesses there are, what treatment are intended to accomplish, under what circumstances, and how they are to be utilized more fully. Related to these basic issues is our need as a people to integrate both our medical delivery system under *our* national health insurance program with social service program account and income maintenance program account available to all populations in our society.

## REFERENCES

Bremmer, M. Harvey. *Mental Illness and the Economy.* Cambridge, Mass.: Harvard University Press.

Ciarlo, James A., and Jacqueline Reihman. *Development of a Multi-Dimensional Program Evaluation Instrument* Mental Health Systems Evaluation Project of the Northwest Denver Mental Health Center and the University of Denver.

Fishman, Daniel B. *Development and Test of a Cost-Effectiveness Methodology for CMHCS,* Contract No. HSM–42–73–162 (OP). Washington, D.C.: U.S. Department of Health, Education, and Welfare.

Foley, Henry A. 1972. *Financing Mental Health Care and Related Social Services.* Delivered at NIMH Regional Funding Conference, Austin, Tex.

*Financing Mental Health Care in the United States: A Study and Assessment of Issues and Arrangements.* 1973. Washington, D.C.: The Advisory Panel on Financing Mental Health Care, American Hospital Association, National Institute of Mental Health.

Hall, Charles P., Jr. 1971. *Third Party Payments: Current Resources—Directions for the Future.* Delivered at NIMH Regional Funding Conference, Chicago, Ill.

*Insurance for Mental Health: Trends in the Delivery and Financing of Mental Illness Services in the United States.* 1974. Report of the Work Group on Health Insurance. Washington, D.C.: National Institute of Mental Health.

Levine, Daniel S. and Dianne R. Levine. 1974. *The Cost of Mental Illness.* Prepared for the National Institute of Mental Health, Contract No. ADM–42–74–82 (OP). Washington, D.C.: U.S. Department of Health, Education and Welfare.

National Conference on Social Welfare. Institute on Health and Health Care Delivery. 1975. *The Impact of National Health Insurance on Services to the Mentally Ill and Mentally Disabled.* Preliminary report of the Task Force in conjunction with the 102nd Annual Forum, San Francisco, May 10–May 16.

Reed, Louis S., Evelyn S. Myers, and Patricia L. Scheidemandel. 1972. *Health Insurance and Psychiatric Care; Utilization and Cost.* (Baltimore Garamond/Pridemark Press 1972).

Scharfstein, Steven S., and Howard L. Magnas. 1975. *Insuring Intensive Psychotherapy.* Paper prepared for presentation to the American Psychiatric Association, Anaheim, Calif.

U.S. Congress. House of Representatives. Committee on Post Office and Civil Service, Sub-committee on Retirement and Employee Benefits. 1974. *Utilization of Mental Health Benefits Under the Federal Employees' Program.* Hearings, 93rd Congress, 2nd Session, September 16 and October 8, 1974. Data reported by Blue Cross–Blue Shield and Aetna Life and Casualty Federal Employee Programs. Washington, D.C.: U.S. Government Printing Office.

U.S. Congress. Senate. Committee on Government Operations, Permanent Subcommittee on Investigations. 1974. *Defense Department's CHAMPUS Program.* Hearings, 93rd Congress, 2nd Session, July 23 and 24, 1974. Washington, D.C.: U.S. Government Printing Office.

# Chapter Ten

# Conclusion

*Robert J. Westlake*

We have viewed the problem of improving the distribution of mental health services in America from several perspectives. Each preceding chapter has presented the position of a nationally known spokesman for one of the major interest groups in our current health care scene. Emerging from these positions is a general consensus that improvement in mental health distribution is desirable but also the accompanying realization in the way in which such improvements are made will have important ramifications for our society, and for the mental health field.

Many faults in our current delivery system have been clearly identified and suggestions for possible changes have been made, but in most cases the suggestions raise more questions than they answer. A brief listing of some of these questions demonstrates their fundamental and complex nature:

Does the public value the treatment of emotional illness as highly as other medical programs with which psychiatric care will compete for a share of the national health care dollar?

Is the public well enough informed to make a decision on these matters and if not, how can they best be informed?

Is the consumer of mental health services actually better served in countries such as Canada and England where a system of equal access to treatment has already been developed?

Would psychiatric treatment without appreciable charge to the patient be "overutilized"?

Would adherance to the "medical model" of psychiatry (to which insurors seem drawn) stifle the development of alternate treatment models?

Could a program of totally insured psychiatric care be grafted on-to our current delivery system without a major revision of that system?

The answers to some of these difficult questions may be found in a careful study of the structure of our American social and economic systems while other answers must be sought in psychiatric theory and current modes of practice. In offering preliminary solutions, it has become clear that if government and insurors are to be able to provide a wide range of mental health services to every citizen, providers will have to find some way to clarify what they do (i.e., provide workable definitions of mental illness and treatment) and to provide reasonable measures of efficacy of such treatment. Insurors, government, and providers have each shown considerable responsibility in working towards these goals within their own systems but at this time a truly collaborative effort is required if there is to be significant and responsible change.

Many of the chapters have presented a cautious attitude towards major intervention in the delivery system for mental health services. It has been noted that while our current system is faulty and has evolved in an unplanned fashion, it has some basic strengths. Past experiences with some health legislation has shown us that desired modifications in health care delivery are not easily achieved. It is not at all certain that a total mental health care system which is the product of careful social design would in fact deliver better services or be more acceptable to the public than our current system.

At this time, legislative commitment for an all encompassing system of national health insurance seems to have moderated. An air of caution prevails which suggests a slowdown in the development of federal legislation enabling broader service delivery and perhaps a continuation of the current trend for legislation which provides increasing controls on already existing programs. We may well have a national health insurance bill before the end of this decade, but the shape of that bill, the degree to which it will be all encompassing or more "catastrophic" in its focus, and the degree to which it will include adequate mental health benefits are all in doubt.

In this evolving situation with forces and counterforces, demands for services, and fiscal realities opposing each other, there remains a persistent public impetus for some change in health care delivery.

Our governmental system dictates that the final decision on the allocation of limited health care dollars and resources will be political in nature. If we wish to affect the outcome of the national health care debate, mental health professionals must understand the dynamic forces operating and to be willing to come forward with a vigorous advocacy role formulating proposals and developing a broadly endorsed plan for inclusion in national legislation.

The fact that the total situation has not yet gelled has important implications for those interested in the inclusion of mental health benefits. For various psychological and political reasons, mental health benefits could be easily overlooked, eliminated, or severely restricted in a political compromise and these benefits are very vulnerable. It is therefore doubly important that the mental health profession adopt a role of political involvement in order to help our nation retain its leadership in quality of care while at the same time providing a long overdue remedy for the disparity in availability of mental health services.

This volume is intended as an introduction to the field and as an in-depth examination of several viewpoints at a given moment in our history. The importance of the relationship between mental health services and their method of funding suggestions that additional research is needed to investigate proposed solutions and to scientifically test hypotheses which have been offered. It is hoped that providers, insurors, government, and public advocacy groups will responsibly collaborate in this research so that the results may be brought to bear upon the political decisions that will eventually shape our mental health delivery system.

# About the Author

Robert J. Westlake, M.D., is Associate Professor of Psychiatry at Brown University and Director of the Outpatient Division of Butler Hospital. He received his medical degree at the University of Pennsylvania and his psychiatric training at the New York State Psychiatric Institute and the Institute of the Pennsylvania Hospital. He has written on Psychiatry and the Law and other interface issues affecting mental health service delivery. He was the organizer of the Butler Hospital Symposium entitled, "Shaping the Future: Planning and Funding for Mental Health Care."